# TOWN PLANNING
## IN ANCIENT DEKKAN

# TOWN PLANNING
## IN ANCIENT DEKKAN


BY

**C. P. VENKATARAMA AYYAR,** M.A., L. T.,

***Reader in Dravidian Philology in the University of Madras.***
***Author of "A Critical Study of tirumurukarruppadai";***
***"Youth and Character"; "Kamban and His Art", etc.***



WITH AN INTRODUCTION BY

**PROFESSOR PATRICK GEDDES**

***Director of the Cities and Town Planning Exhibition.***

*Published by*

Gyan Publishing House
5, Ansari Road
Daryaganj, New Delhi-110002
Phone: 011-47034999, 9811692060
E-mail: books@gyanbooks.com

*Distribution Network*
gyanbooks.com
India, USA, Canada, UK, Australia, France



ISBN : 978-81-212-4135-9 (PB)
First Published, 1916

2nd Impression 2021

*Printed at:* Gyan Press, Delhi.



**Town Planning in Ancient Dekkan**
Author: C. P. Venkatarama Ayyar

# TOWN PLANNING

## IN ANCIENT DEKKAN

BY

C. P. VENKATARAMA AYYAR, M.A., L.T.,

*Reader in Dravidian Philology in the University of Madras.*

*Author of "A Critical Study of Tirumurukāṟṟuppaḍai"; "Youth and Character"; "Kamban and his Art", etc.*

WITH AN INTRODUCTION BY

PROFESSOR PATRICK GEDDES,

*Director of the Cities and Town Planning Exhibition.*

---

MADRAS:

PRINTED AT THE LAW PRINTING HOUSE

MOUNT ROAD.

General view of the Temple with the Towers—Tirukkaḻukkunṟam (page 167).

To

Brihma Sri Mahamahopadhyaya

**V. SWAMINATHA AYYAR, AVL.,**

Tamil Pandit, Presidency College, Madras

But for whose invaluable labour of love in the field of ancient Tamil literature for a period extending over forty years, the best classics which mirror the ancient culture and civilisation of the people would not have been recovered from oblivion and resuscitated for the benefit of the present generation and posterity ; and to whom belongs unquestionably the high merit of having re-awakened an interest in and given an impetus to the study of ancient Tamil classics

THIS BOOK

IS

**DEDICATED**

as a humble token of highest regard and gratitude

**BY THE AUTHOR**

A former pupil of the Pandit and a Tamil Prizeman of the Presidency College.

# PREFACE.

When Professor Geddes was lecturing in Madras on the subject of town planning my valued friend M. R. Ry., Rao Bahadur C. V. Muniswamy Ayyar Avargal of the *Madras Mail* suggested to me the desirability of examining the classical Tamil literature to find out any references to the town planning of Indian cities that this may contain, and prepare an essay on the subject and send it to the talented Professor. I accordingly prepared a short note on the subject, and forwarded it to the Professor, who, on receiving the paper, advised me to elaborate and publish it in book form as early as possible.

The following pages were thus inspired by the advice so kindly given by the Professor and the encouragement that this literary endeavour in a wide field of research in ancient culture and civilisation, received at his hands. Throughout this book, the aim has been to make literature speak for itself. Nothing has been adduced but what has been proved by the literary excerpts quoted in the footnotes. Extracts from the most ancient Tamil literature wherever they throw light on the principles of town planning have been collected together. The entire body of Tamil literature which bear on the subject of town or village planning and sanitation is very vast. And only a few of the more important literary illustrations selected from the standard classics in Tamil, and bearing on the topic have been picked out and examined here.

In the use of such literary material for the purpose, I may at once answer a few criticisms that are generally offered. A few critics hold that the poets display exuberant imagination and that the descriptions of cities in books would not therefore conform to actualities. They wish to find minute descriptions of form and shape in literature. This is ignoring the distinction between the product of a poet's art and the treatise written by a scientist. The scientific temper observes all things with a view to discover their mode of existence, their relations to each other and to the environment. But the literary temper observes such things in their relation to man's emotional and moral nature. The poet does not therefore weave out of a fertile imagination but he simply describes what pleasurable feelings the external objects rouse in him. And to this extent, his literary temper is not incompatible with the scientific. As our esteemed countryman the Hon'ble Sir P. S. Sivaswami Ayyar, K.C.S.I., C.I.E., so clearly put it, "It would be absurd to suppose that such descriptions of cities and towns in literature were not founded on a solid substratum of truth."

Other critics of Indian literature state that the descriptions are stereotyped and as such do not portray actual facts. This sweeping remark, though born of ignorance or prejudice, calls for an answer. In every literature under the sun, we find periods dominated by the "correct school" with the concomitant result of the crushing out of all natural singing of the true poets. The artificial high sounding lines of the poetry of Dryden and Pope in English literature failed to catch the note of primitive wonder and substituted instead an impulse of unquestioning acceptance. There are such periods in Tamil literature also but they are comparatively very recent. Some recent Tamil Puranas betray some such convention. But such a charge could not be levelled against the poetry of the remote past, the ancient Tamil classics. This is full of wonder which attacks the external forms with open eyes of enquiry.

Some other critics deplore the absence of a definite chronology which would give us clear ideas of the principles of Town Planning. A chronology of the more ancient poets has mainly to be settled by internal evidence, such as style, meanings of words, concordance and so on. In the present state of Vernacular study it would be many years before such a History of Tamil literature becomes an accomplished fact. A chronology would no doubt be a valuable aid to historical studies but the absence of it does not militate against the accuracy of the principles of Town Planning which literature reveals. And further, these principles seem to be the same throughout, the essential difference in ideals being apparent only in the objects sought to be attained by cities, such as temple cities and fortified cities.

The question whether the civilization of the South is purely Dravidian or purely Aryan or whether it is a blend of the two is a very big one which I do not at present propose to discuss. There are some treatises in Tamil on the subject of architecture and until they are critically studied, one might not venture opinions on such interesting points. In the meanwhile we need not be deterred from diving into the Tamil classics to see what ideas the ancient Tamils had on the subject.

The word Dekkan is used in this book in the sense in which it is ordinarily understood in these parts as a Tamil Tadbhava form of the Sanskrit word Daksinam meaning South, *i.e.*, South India.

What I have here attempted is thus an account of the details of the town plan of some of the more important cities in the Tamil country. Incidentally the characteristic features of Indian cities, the endeavour of people to so execute the planning as to conduce to efficiency in health and comfort, the attempts made off and on to rebuild cities or otherwise extend them to meet growing demands have been examined. And in the account of the building of the towns, the original ideas that brought them into being have been stated in order that the essential principles which the ancient Tamils had in view on the subject may be presented in their true perspective.

The method followed in examining the subject is the least exceptionable. The intimate connection subsisting between literature and culture is an axiomatic truth. The national literature of any country is but the expression of the changing life of the nation that has produced it. For literature is one side of history and often its most instructive side. An intimate familiarity with ancient Tamil classics is thus helfpful in giving us an insight into the spirit that underlay the external life of the Tamils of ancient days. And in as much as these books mirror the spirit of the age in which they were produced, they are most valuable records of ancient life and manners.

Many of the noblest writings of this sort lay buried in cadjan manuscripts for several years past and were a prey to white ants. Happily for the country, M.R.Ry. Pandit Mahamahopadhyaya Swaminatha Ayyar Avargal began, some four decades ago, the study and examination of these manuscripts in a spirit of research. The manuscripts lay scattered and uncared for in stray houses in remote villages and his diligent search and study aided by an inborn spirit of research and literary acumen have enabled him to publish the valuable masterpieces of ancient literature, which have been a forgotten but priceless inheritance of the Tamils for several centuries. The student of ancient culture and civilisation cannot therefore be too grateful to this talented scholar and pioneer of Tamil research in India.

The books published by the Mahamahopadhaya have been chiefly laid under contribution in the following pages. The references to these and other works are given in the footnotes as such references were regarded as an essential part of the work, as with them, the value of the evidence on the question of town planning is practically removed from the domain of imagination and bias, and placed upon the sure ground of a literary and historic reflection of the real life of the ancient Tamils, thus facilitating easy reference to the original extracts quoted in the following pages. Most of the literary excerpts quoted herein are from classics which date as far back as the 1st century A.D. References to later literature are very few, as the aim is to give a correct view of the civic ideals of the more ancient times. Hence the question has been dealt with from the purely Hindu point of view, the Muhammadan period belonging to the mediæval epoch.

This book is thus an exposition of the aims of the builders of Madura, Conjeeveram and other ancient cities, and if it should, even in a small measure help to make one realise the principles underlying the planning of such cities as examples of how best to secure objects, which make town life tolerable to people and thereby promote conditions, the absence of which spells a menace to the vitality of the population, it would have achieved the purpose for which it was published.

In bringing out this publication, I cannot adequately express my deep gratitude to **Professor Patrick Geddes of the University of St. Andrews** who, from the very beginning, when I showed my manuscripts to him, evinced a sympathetic interest in this humble literary endeavour and encouraged me by advice, suggestion and his valuable Introduction. As the author of the Kural says in Tamil,

> "*செய்யாமற் செய்த வுதவிக்கு வையகமும்*
> *வானகமு மாற்ற லரிது.*"

"A benefit conferred, where none has been received

Is greater worth than ever could be achieved

By giving heaven and earth." (Gover's Translation).

C.P.V.

## ABBREVIATIONS.

Ch.—Chapter.

L.—Line.

V.—Verse.

## BIBLIOGRAPHY.

Ac.—Ātticcūḍi—ஆத்திச்சூடி.

Br.—Brahmōttara Kāṇḍam } பிரமோத்தர காண்டம்.

Cin.—Cintāmaṇi—சிந்தாமணி.

Cl.—N.—Cūḷāmaṇi—சூளாமணி—நகரப்படலம்.

Kall.—Kallāḍam—கல்லாடம்.

Kam.—Kamba Rāmāyaṇam—கம்பராமாயணம்.

Kanci.—Kāncippurāṇam—காஞ்சிப்புராணம்.

Kanda.—C.—Kandapurāṇam } கந்தபுராணம் சூர நகர்.

Kanda.—N.—Kandapurāṇam Nāṭṭuppaḍalam } கந்தபுராணம் நாட்டுப்படலம்.

Kanda.—Nakar—Kandapurā-ṇam, Nakarappaḍalam } கந்தபுராணம் நகரப்படலம்.

Kon.—Konṛaivēndan—கொன்றைவேந்தன்.

Kural.—Kuṛaḷ—திருக்குறள்.

Mad.—Maduraikkāñci—மதுரைக் காஞ்சி.

Man.—Maṇimēkalai—மணிமேகலை.

M. V. P.—Manai Vīṭṭupporu-ttam } மனை வீட்டுப் பொருத்தம்.

N.—Naisadam—நைஷதம்.

Nal.—Nāladiyār—நாலடியார்.

Ne.—Neḍunalvāḍai—நெடுநல்வாடை.

Nik.—Nikaṇḍu—நிகண்டு.

Nv.—Nalvaḻi—நல்வழி.

Nvb.—Nītiveṇbā—நீதிவெண்பா.

O. T.—Old Tiruviḷaiyāḍal Purāṇam—வேம்பத்தூரார்த் திருவிளையாடற்புராணம்.

Pattin.—Paṭṭinappālai—பட்டினப்பாலை.

Periya.—Periya Purāṇam—பெரிய புராணம்.

Perum.—Perumpāṇāṟṟuppaḍai—பெரும்பாணாற்றுப்படை.

Por.—Porunarāṟṟuppaḍai—பொருநராற்றுப்படை.

Pur.—Puṟanāṉūṟu—புறநானூறு.

P. T.—Paranjoti Munivar's Tiruviḷaiyāḍal Purāṇam—பரஞ்சோதி முனிவர் திருவிளையாடற் புராணம்.

Sil.—Śilappadikāram—சிலப்பதிகாரம்.

Sir.—Śiṟupāṇaṟṟuppaḍai—சிறுபாணாற்றுப்படை.

Tev.—Tēvāram—தேவாரம்.

Tir.—Tirukkuṟipputtoṇḍanār Purāṇam—திருக்குறிப்புத் தொண்டனார் புராணம்.

Tiru.—Tirumurukāṟṟuppaḍai—திருமுருகாற்றுப்படை.

Tml.—Tiruvāimoḻi—திருவாய்மொழி

Tnl.—Tirunāḷaippōvār Purāṇam—திருநாளைப்போவார் புராணம்.

Tol.—Tolkāppiyam—தொல்காப்பியம் (p. 8).

Vet.—Veṟṟivēṟkai—வெற்றி வேற்கை.

## *ERRATA.*

P. 9, ll. 6, 19—*for* Coimbatore *read* Trichinopoly

P. 52, l. 23—*for* யாக்குஞ் *read* யாக்கு.

## CONTENTS.



## ILLUSTRATIONS.

# INTRODUCTION.

I had the good fortune first to make the acquaintance of Mr. Venkatarama Ayyar at Madras in 1914 as a learned translator and commentator of the Town Planning lore of the Tamil Shastras, which I hope he will some day publish. But he is right in preparing the public by this more popular volume with its bright revival of the ancient glories of South India civilisation. The hard scientific reader may at times grimly recall that the statistics of sacred and classic literatures are usually in generous and rounded figures, and that ancient glories do not lose in the telling. But when all reasonable scepticism is allowed for, the main impression of the book is unshaken—for ancient glories there were; and these on a scale exceeding not only our modern wealth and well-being, or the modest hopes of our social improvers, but even the constructions of our would be Utopia-makers. That India, and particularly South India, was, and this up to a not so remote past, one of the greatest city-making regions of the world, is ever being more plainly re-established by the investigators of books and of buildings alike; and I have been fully convinced also by my own eyes.

At this time especially there is use,—impulse and hope also,—in such a vivid and popular presentment of ancient city life as this of Mr. Venkatarama Ayyar's. Had the present or recent Town Councils of Madura for instance, been acquainted with it, they would not so readily have joined in the sanitary panic of the tank-destroyer; not so readily have allowed the rise of some of the worst slums of India, and not so meekly have surrendered the ground which is urgently needed for the city's extension to hospital and college and Collector's Offices and what not—uses all doubtless excellent by themselves, but as well or better satisfied further afield. A younger generation of councillors, with their ancestral memories stirred by this book, will see their responsibilities and powers with more open eyes, and their British collaborators with them, and so in other cities of South India, and beyond.

PATRICK GEDDES.

CITIES AND TOWN
PLANNING EXHIBITION,
LUCKNOW.
*22nd March, 1916.*

# TOWN PLANNING
# IN ANCIENT DEKKAN.

## CHAPTER I.

### ORIGIN OF CITIES.

Of all things which men have imagined, the town is perhaps the noblest. From very early times, men's thoughts have been directed to the town, as a centre of civilisation and as a refuge in times of war. Cities evolve quite naturally, and unconsciously. But there are also cities which have been consciously founded for definite ends.

Of cities which have evolved unconsciously, it may be mentioned that certain natural advantages like a sea-coast, a river valley and so on, mostly favour their growth. In India cities have mostly grown round temples. People are attracted in large numbers to places which have become famous on account of a temple. And where people congregate, trade and commerce flourish, civilisation spreads, and cities in the real sense of the word naturally evolve. Thus the mutual attraction, *viz.*, of temples to natural surroundings, and of cities to temples have been the chief factors in the growth and development of city life in India.

As the great poetess, Avvaiyār has said [1] "One should not live in a place which does not possess a temple.' For the existence of a temple implies sanctity and hence sanitation of the surroundings, an assured water supply, a flower-garden, a modest byre for supplying milk to the temple, and other amenities of life which one values most.

It is remarkable that spirituality and morality, cleanliness and Godliness, commerce and religion interact on one another in the social well-being of the people.

---

1 கோயிலில்லா ஊரிற் குடியிருக்க வேண்டாம்.

The great shrines in India, which as centres of pilgrimage attract a large concourse of people, are almost always associated with some great and beautiful manifestation of Nature. The spots which are thus most favoured by the Gods are aptly described by the poet Nakkīrar in exquisite lines which forcibly bring before the mind's eye the infinite and the sublime in Nature. The poet says[2] "God is pleased to preside in each and every village and town where feasts are solemnly observed in His honour; where the real devotee concentrates his mind upon HIM; where a place is sanctified for HIS worship; in forests, in groves, and in islands created by the confluence of rivers, on river banks, tank bunds and generally in all

---

2 ஊரூர் கொண்ட சீர்கெழு விழவினும்
ஆர்வலர் ஏத்த மேவரு நிலையினும்
வேலன் றைஇய வெறியயர் களனும்
காடுங் காவுங் கவின்பெறு துருத்தியும்
யாறுங் குளனும் வேறுபல் வைப்புஞ்
சதுக்கமுஞ் சந்தியும் புதுப்பூங் கடம்பு
மன்றமும் பொதியிலுங் கந்துடை நிலையினும்

(Tiru.—220-226).

places of public worship in squares in the heart of towns; where three streets and five streets meet; in public halls and under the shade of trees planted in the centre of a village and surrounded by a platform where all people could meet; and in cow-houses provided with a central rough stone against which the cows could rub their bodies."

These lines furnish the key to the proper understanding of the principles underlying the selection of sites for the building of temples and of cities which follow in their wake. The limitless expanse of the wide ocean with its unceasing dash of waves against the shore, the meandering course of great rivers, the estuary where the rivers empty their contents into a sea which does not seem to be too full for all the waters it receives, and the confluence of mighty rivers, bring before the minds of the people as no other circumstance could bring, that conscious sense of the infinite in face of the finite, which is of the very essence of all religions. A stately temple rising against the sky, high gopurams or entrance to temples, a vast sheet of water surrounded by grand temples which cast their reflection on the transparent surface below and such other conditions envelop a place in an atmosphere of sanctity and incidentally promote the health conscience of the people.

Thus the beginnings of cities are to be found in the importance of religious worship and in the pilgrimage to shrines, which form a notable feature in the life of the Indian nation generally. If cities grow around sites which have become famous on account of their sacred associations, it is none the less true that people flock to centres of commerce, sites the admirable situation of which ensure an unfailing supply of abundant food material for all classes, and places which also afford protection against surprise in war. A clear coast-belt, or a natural river or hill boundary are alike easy of access in times of peace and easy of defence in times of war. And when one remembers the incessant feuds among the ancient Tamil Kingdoms of the South, the fact is clear that such spots were selected for commerce, for civilisation and for defence as well by reason of the natural facilities they offered for all these purposes.

Cities have thus an unconscious or a conscious growth. And taking all facts into consideration one might venture to say even at this distant date whether a particular city was the outcome of unconscious evolution or of conscious creation. Though people are attracted to a place quite unconsciously and naturally in the beginning, the conscious planning and development of the city for definite purposes, soon began to play an important part in the growth of such cities.

Of the cities that have been here taken up for study, Madura, Vanji, Conjeevaram and Kavēripūmpaṭṭinam and Woraiyur, the last at any rate was a conscious and deliberate creation of the Chola King, Cholan Karikāl Peruvaḷaṭṭān who had his capital in Kavēripūmpaṭṭinam for a very long time.

There can be no doubt whatever about the antiquity of these cities. They are the most ancient cities in South India and they are described in full in the literature of the country. Such descriptions touch upon several points of the details of town planning which are very material for a proper understanding of the principles the ancients had in view in the building of cities.

### *Madura.*

Madura was well known to the Greeks and Romans of ancient days. The city is mentioned in Ptolemy's Tables as the seat of the Pandian Kingdom in the South. The Greek name for the city of Madura is MODOURA. It is also known as Kaḍambavana, *i.e.*, the forest of Kaḍamba trees (Anthocephalus Kaḍamba). There is a tradition that a forest was here cleared to extend the limits of the city. The city naturally rose in importance on account of the fertility of the Vaikai valley, the defence provided by the river Vaikai on one side and by the sea on two other sides, the east and the south; and above all by the magnificent temple of Mīnākshi Sundarēsvara, the central diadem of the Tamil land in the description and praise of which poets have vied with one another. It was the cradle of the Tamil Muse and to it all votaries of Tamil learning went from different parts of the Tamil country, from the Vēnkata hills on the north to Cape Comorin on the south,[3] and from the Bay of Bengal on the east to the Arabian sea on the west. Arts and letters thus flourished in this ancient city which was also a great centre of trade and the central seat of Government. Vanji was the ancient capital of the Chera Kings as Madura was the capital of the Pandian Kings. It is also known as Karoor. (Greek name Karoura Basileios Kerobotros) the ancient capital of the Chera Kings. The site of this ancient city is now a deserted village near Cochin. In this village are still to be seen some remains of an old temple and other old buildings which are well worth exploring

---

3 வடவேங்கடந்தென்குமரி
ஆயிடை தமிழ் கூறு நல்லுலகம்

into for historical materials which may lie buried there.

There is also another city known as Karour which is also reputed to have been the capital of the Chera country. This is the modern Karur in the Coimbatore district. This is different from the old city of Vanji or Karur above described. A prince of the Chera dynasty who once ruled over those parts constructed a city on the plan of the ancient city of Vanji with which he was very familiar. From the standpoint of town planning and the growth of cities this is equally interesting to us. The selection of the site and the other details of planning enable us to understand the main principles in the evolution of cities.

The new city of Karur in the Coimbatore District which was planned on the lines of the ancient city of Karur (Vanji in Cochin), and named after that ancient capital is situated on rising ground on the left bank of the *Amravaty* and near its confluence with the Cauvery. It has an ancient temple dedicated to Siva (Pasupateswara). It was an important frontier post between Trichinopoly and the old Mysore territory and was the scene of several military movements in ancient times. Here also we find that the vicinity of the river, the old shrine, the elevation and the strategic position on the Mysore frontier were the natural advantages, which, aided by a strong fort and other artificial contrivances, contributed to the growth of the city and its influence as a centre of culture in ancient times.

Conjeevaram is one of the seven holy cities of India and of equal importance with ancient cities like Oudh and Benares. This is the KIEN-CHI-PU-LO described by Hwen Thsang as a great Buddhist centre when he visited it. The general level of the city rises gradually from the river Palar to the north and the west. The Palar and the Vegavati rivers contribute to the fertility of the valley. The city has also in it an ancient Siva Temple which is the largest and the oldest and a notable Vishnu Temple. The numerous other temples dedicated to Kāmākshi, Subramaniya and other deities filled a large space in the town which is from five to six miles long and has broad streets well planted with avenue trees. Here also as in other cities considered above, the rivers, the temple, the fertility of the plain, etc., have been greatly responsible for its selection as the central seat of Government of the ancient Kings of Thoṇḍaināḍu.

Woraiyur which is two miles from Trichinopoly was a city newly planned and built by the great Chola King, Karikāl Peruvaḷattān. This was a conscious creation of a city occupied for administrative purposes as the seat of Government by the Chola Kings. This was also an ancient city. The Greek name is Orthura Basileios Sornagos. It is known also as Koḻiyur or the city of the Fowl. The story goes that when once the Chola King went out on his elephant into the forest there, a fowl attacked the elephant boldly. The king was astonished that an ordinary fowl should have summoned courage to attack an elephant.

So struck was he with the incident that he paused to make a local inspection of the spot which led him to the conclusion that the site was eminently fit to build a town. He[4] then resolved to build a city on the site which he thought must be a very fertile area as even the fowls gained greatly in strength and valour when brought up on such a spot. So enchanted was he by the beauty of the situation and the salubrity of its air that the King decided that it was a most desirable place for the erection of his palace, and forrearing a city around. With this idea he first of all cleared the forest and after a clean deforestation[5] of the area he dug out many

---

4 முரஞ்செவி வாரணம் முன்சம முருக்கிய
புறஞ்சிறை வாரணம் புக்கனர் புரிந்தென.

(Sil.—IX—247-248).

5 காடு கொன்று நாடாக்கிக்
குளந் தொட்டு வளம் பெருக்கிப்
பிறங்கு நிலைமாடத் துறந்தை போக்கிக்
கோயிலொடு குடி நிறீஇ
வாயிலொடு புழை யமைத்து
ஞாயிறொறும் புதை நிறீஇ.

(Pattin. 283-289).

tanks, constructed a beautiful mansion for himself and houses for others; built a fine temple in the centre and established the several castes in several areas, built a fort with walls around, and with a grand entrance in front, and a small gateway behind; and mounted on the ramparts of the fort all the necessary defences for guarding the city against surprise attacks. He then directed the people to live there. The town flourished in all splendour as the capital of the Chola King. The alluvial deposits of the Cauvery which ensured an unfailing supply of water for irrigation and domestic purposes all the year round, the easy inland communication by means of the river and the defence afforded by the same, contain all the elements which go to make a fine city. The provision of food grains in abundance from a fertile tract, fish from the river, easy defence in times of war, good inland communication for commerce, and lastly the most important ancient temples of Siva and Vishnu, marked it as a great and considerable city.

The commanding view of the great rock rising to a height of nearly 275 feet from the plain in the centre of Trichinopoly and towering above the surrounding country as a sentinel for miles around, the river Coleroon leaving the parent stream and bringing into existence the island of Srirangam around which it passes as a pearl necklace about the golden shrine of Sri Ranganatha and clothed by green verdure on either bank present a sight which is a feast to the eyes. The deforestation of areas, the rearing of cities and the environing by fortifications of newly-built cities for definite purposes, undertaken by the Chola King, are evidences of the high state of civilisation reached by the Tamils in those ancient times.

Coming to the important city of Kāvēripūmpaṭṭinam here also there is an ancient shrine dedicated to Siva Pallavaneswarar.[6] This is a very ancient city

---

6 மந்தலாய மல்லிகையும் புன்னைவளர்குரவின்
பந்தலாரும் பட்டினத்துப் பல்லவனீச்சரமே.

(Tev.—I).

which was once a flourishing sea-port and a great centre of commerce. It is the Khabiros Emporion of the Greeks. The Tamil name means the Kaveri town. It is also known as Pukār[7] or the city at the mouth of the Kavery. It had a splendid harbour and a lighthouse. This ancient sea-port which had an extensive commerce has ceased to be of importance owing to the silting up of the Kavery. Nothing now remains of the once famed city except a few sandy mounds with fragments of bricks and some traces of temples and old wells near.

This ancient city stood on a spot about 9 miles to the south-east of Shiyali in the Tanjore district of the Madras Presidency. And though it is now completely destroyed, the description of the city in the literature of the land shows what a great and considerable sea-port it was in those ancient times. The plan of the town, the distribution of the several castes and

---

7 பழியிலார்கள் பயில் புகார்.

(Tev.—I).

occupational groups in well planned areas in the town, and the life of the citizens, are all most graphically described in an ancient Tamil classic, Silappadikaram.

Thus these great cities are pointed out again and again in ancient Tamil classics as model cities[8] worth our attention—Madura for its lofty mansions and high buildings; Woraiyur for superb excellence in everything that contributes to healthy civic life; Vanji for its commercial prosperity; and Pukār or Kāvēripūmpaṭṭinam at the mouth of the Kavery for its excellent natural harbour which secured safe anchorage for merchant vessels.

When one remembers that town planning is a growing art and that the life of every town is a continual change, a constant building afresh and extension to meet growing demands, the conclusion is irresistible that the fame of the cities

8 மாட மதுரையும் பீடா ருறந்தையும்
கலிகெழு வஞ்சியும் ஒலிபுனற் புகாரும்.
(Sil.—VIII—3-4).

should have become so well and so long established and should have been so wide-spread as to have attracted the attention of the early classical writers of the west, whose reference in glowing terms to these cities has been responsible for drawing the adventurous spirits amongst the early Greeks and Romans to come and settle in these eastern cities as traders and as mercenary troops at so early a period as the 1st and 2nd century A. D.

---

# CHAPTER II.

## THE GROWTH OF CITIES.

The growth of cities has always been from within. Under the old system ample provision was made for the extension of cities according as the need for such extension became pressing. In this connection it is well worth noticing that *Nakar* the Tamil word for city is used variously in ancient Tamil Literature to mean [1] a house, a temple, a palace or a castle, and a city.

---

1 பைஞ்சேறு மெழுகிய படிவ நன்னகர் (house)
(Perum.—l. 298).
பொன்துஞ்சு வியனகர் (palace)
(Perum.—l. 440).
அரூஅ யாணர் வளங்கெழு திருநகர் (city)
(Mad.—l. 169).
நடுஊர் நகர் (Temple)
(Kall.—v.-14).
பொன்னகர்க் கூடல் சென்னியம் பிறையோன் (mansion)
(Kall.--v.-3).

A city proper meant a collection of houses built in various localities to accommodate several classes of people according to their station. Separate houses make up a town just as separate men make up a people. Where people congregated for a common end, the collection of houses in a locality gave rise to the formation of a city. In temple cities, the temple was the centre or starting point round which grew up the city. And likewise a palace or a castle was the starting point in the building of fortified cities. The expansion was thus from within.

### *Nakar.*

The word 'nakar' which is thus used to indicate at once a house, a palace, a temple, and a city contains in a nut-shell, the chief dynamic principle of ancient town planning, that these separate items should be so co-ordinated and each assigned such an important place in the city that the arrangement conduces to the efficiency of town life.

To every householder, his house is his own castle of which he is the sole lord;

and it is also his own temple where he instals in a sanctified place, his own family deity and worships that deity.

Again the word contains a great truth as regards the sentiments of loyalty to the Sovereign which is the basic principle of good citizenship. That the same word 'nakar' is used to mean a temple and a palace, shows that the residential quarters of the king were looked upon with a veneration as great as the temple of God. The person of the king and everything pertaining to him has always been sacrosanct with the Indian people. As a Tamil Saint has said "Kings are the accredited representatives of the manifestation of God-head as a protector". The Hindu belief being that there is no king without an element of Vishnu (the protecting God of the Trinity) in him, the same amount of regard and veneration is due to him as is due to God.[2]

The same word 'Koil' represents a

---

2 திருவுடை மன்னரைக் காணில் திருமாலைக் கண்டேனே யென்னும் (Tml.—4—4).

palace and a temple or a place of worship. Thus the history of these words embody a moral idea. The notions of loyalty which these words connote are quite characteristic of the Indian mind from time immemorial.

*The nucleus of a city.*

Thus taking the palace or the temple as a starting point, houses are built around them and the city grows gradually and expands. In the case of a temple city, there were four streets about the temple where the priests and other servants of the temple had their residential quarters. We gather from the Purāṇās or local traditions that in Conjeeveram the priests of the temple were accommodated in the four streets [3] round the temple.

[3] இருண்மலந் துமிக்குஞ் சிவாகம முறையினீரு
பாதமு மனுட்டித்
தருள்பெறு மாதி சைவர்க ளாதி யவாந்தர
சைவரீ ருணோர்
மருவிவாழ் மாடமாளிகைப் பத்தி மருங்குடுத்
துயர்வனப் பினதாற்
றெருடருமணுதி சைவர்வீற் றிருக்குந் திவ
ளொளிப் புரிசையே சம்பம்
(Kanci.—Nak.-v.-110).

The four streets round the temple were also used for processional purposes. These streets round the temple which encloses the noble mango tree under whose luxuriant umbrage God *Siva* first gave audience to the penitent *Uma*, his Divine Spouse, created practically a square with a large open space, a tank and an orchard tree in the centre.

In the case of a palace, the ministers, the advisers, the soldiers guarding the palace, the rich merchants, and the Brahmins were housed in streets planned round the palace; while the baths, artificial mounds, tanks, orchard and flower gardens, etc., which make palace life pleasant, separated the palace proper from the streets occupied by the ministers and other servants of the Royal household.

The temple or the palace is the nucleus of the village or town round which the houses and other features are grouped. This shows that the lay-out of a village or a city has proceeded on rational lines with reference to the practical requirements of an orderly growth of the houses and of future development of the city. The cottage or the house was fashioned after the human body—the house formed the unit of the village, and the temple or the palace was the starting point for villages and towns alike.

This kind of growth of cities from within, with the temple as a starting point is well indicated in the history of the town planning of the great city of Madura.

# CHAPTER III.

## MADURA.

The town planning of the ancient city of Madura would appear to have been a progressive development from within. The central temple was there from time immemorial and was used as a starting point of measurements when the city was planned.

### *Its Origin.*

The origin of this ancient city as described in the Purāṇās or local traditions is very interesting study. Examined in a critical spirit the Stala Purāṇās or local traditions ought to offer much valuable material for the reconstruction of ancient history and civilisation. One would find that beneath a great deal of mythology there is a solid foundation of historical information and the work in this field would then be productive of a rich harvest of a mass of useful information on various points of historical and antiquarian interest.

The other name for Madura is Kaḍamba Vana or the forest of Kaḍamba trees. The de-forestation of the area and the building of the city of Madura are most graphically described in the Tiruviḷayāḍal Purāṇās in Tamil.

*The first plan.*

Prior to the founding of Madura as it was first planned and built, the Pandian ruler of those times, it is said, had his palace originally in Maṇavūr[1] which lay to the east of the Kaḍamba forests. The Purāṇa also records that while the ruler of the Pandiyan country had his head-quarters in Maṇavūr, a certain rich merchant of the city went bent on trade westwards from the city, with his large merchandise; and that after trading

---

1 கின்னரம் பயில் கடம்பமாவனத்தினின்கீழ் சார்த்
தென்னர் சேகரனெனுங்குல சேகரனுலக
மன்னர் சேகரனரசு செய்திருப்பது மணவூர்.
(P. T.—Ch. 3-v. 2).

in distant countries he returned to his native land laden with riches.[2] On his return-journey, he had still to travel some distance before he could reach his city, when it grew dark and he bethought himself that he might stay somewhere for the night and resume his journey the next morning. Then he came upon an extensive primeval forest consisting mostly of the lordly Kaḍamba trees. He stayed that night in the beautiful Kaḍamba forest. We gather from the Purāṇās that during that night he bathed in a tank in the forest and finished his usual ablutions there. And as he was curious to know what the tank and the forest were like, he carefully studied the surroundings and was surprised to find the emblem of God Śiva in a beautiful spot on the bund of the tank. And when day dawned he was much struck by the beauty of the tank

---

2 செல்வ மாநகரிருந்து மேற்றிசைப் புலஞ் சென்று
மல்லல் வாணிகஞ் செய்துதன் வளம்பதி மீள்
வான்.

(P. T.—Ch. 3-v. 4.)

full of blossoming lotus flowers bathed in the golden rays of the rising sun. His curiosity being roused, he examined the tank and its surroundings more closely than he was able to do on the previous night and found that the emblem of God was overgrown with thick bushes and trees. After bathing in the tank and worshipping the deity in the Kaḍamba forest, he proceeded to Maṇavūr and related to the King the existence of a beautiful tank and temple of God in the forest which lay in the west of the city.

The King was much pleased to hear the glowing account of the merchant about the tank and the temple of God near. So struck was he by the account that he went with his ministers and the merchant to the Kaḍamba forest where the temple was said to exist. And on examining the locality he at once thought that it was a desirable site where he could build a city round the tank and keep the ancient temple of God intact and in its place.

He forthwith directed his ministers to arrange to clear the entire forest and level the ground. Several hundreds of men were employed to fell the forest and the deep and frequent strokes of the woodman's axe[3] was heard for several days.

And when the ground was well cleared and levelled, the King consulted[4] his advisors how best he might plan the city. After much deliberation a plan appears to have been finally evolved and starting with the temple, the main monument in the centre of the proposed city, the King constructed in order, a Padmamaṇḍapam, where the Vedas would be chanted, Ardhamaṇḍapam or the outer hall where festivals might be held, Nṛitta maṇḍapam, the kitchen for the temple, and other

---

3 பாய வேலையினார்த்தனர் வழிக்கொடு படர்ந்தார்
சேய காடெறிந் தணிநகர்செய்தொழின் மாக்கள்.

(P. T.—Ch. 3-v. 26).

4 களைந்து நீணிலந் திருத்திச் செந்நெறி படக்கண்டு
வளைந்து நன்னகரெடுப்ப தெவ்வாறெனா
மந்திரரோ டளைந்தனாவிய சிந்தையோ டிருந்த
னன்.

(P. T.—Ch. 3-v. 32).

small temples around. He then beautified the temple by constructing the grand Gopurams or pyramidal gateways into the temples. The planning of the bazaar streets, the car streets, and the streets for the residential quarters of the several inhabitants next engaged his attention. He also erected some public platforms and planted fruit trees therein. When the streets round the temple (மாடப்பெருந் தெரு) and the chief procession streets (விழாவரு வீதி) have been planned, other small streets intersecting these wide streets were also laid out. And in the open square thus formed, the public meeting place (பொதியில்) and other open places were also planned and constructed. The natural features were utilised to the fullest advantage and the existing streams and ponds were maintained. Some tanks were freshly dug out (தொடு குளம்). The fort walls, ditch, etc., were then planned according to the rules [5] laid down in the

---

5 கம்மிய நூல் தொல்லை வரம்பெல்லை கண்டமைத்தான்.

(P. T.—Ch. 3-v. 38).

śastras of hoary antiquity. Such tanks, orchard gardens, flower gardens, and the moat completed the town plan. The King had his palace [6] constructed in the north-eastern portion of the newly planned city, which was named Madura or the agreeable city [7] as it was conducive to the healthy comfort and prosperity of the people. Such is the history of the origin of the city of Madura, which, the Purāṇa states, was a city planned for definite purposes around an ancient temple. It is here noteworthy that the city building was not made piece by piece and section by section, but as a whole, having regard to the size of the town, the prevention of overcrowding and the provision of open spaces. The whole of the ground was carefully contoured before the town was laid out.

---

6 மாளிகை தனக்கம்மாநகர் வடகுண்பாற் கண்டு

(P. T—Ch. 3-v. 41).

7 மதுர, நன்மயமான தன்மையான் மதுராநகரென வுரைத்தனர் நாமம்

(P. T.—Ch. 3-v. 42).

## *Another Plan.*

The town which was thus planned appears to have had a flourishing existence for a long time when it fell on evil times. For so goes the Purāṇa that it suffered from the devastation of a huge flood from which the ancient temple and its surroundings alone, which were originally on an elevated spot seem to have escaped. These served to house the population which escaped the destruction from the floods, and continued to exist under the appellation of Naḍuvūr[8] or the central place in memory of what was left of the old city after the floods. But as years rolled on Naḍuvūr prospered. And this small strip of land was found insufficient for the needs of a growing

---

8 ஒன்றிய பெருவெள் ளத்து நடுச்சிதையாமலோங்கி
நன்றிய லுலகுக் கெல்லாம் படிமமா நலஞ்சேர்
வெள்ளி
மன்றுடன் விளங்க லாலே மண்மிசை நகர்க்கு நாம
மன்றுமுன் னடுவூ ரென்று· விளங்கிய தமரர்
மெச்ச

(O. T.—Ch. 47-v. 3).

city.[9] The population increased in numbers and the ruler of the day was confronted with the problem of relieving congestion and consequent measures of extension. He then caused a resurvey of the limits of the old city made from a study of the ancient traces with a view to preparing a fresh and comprehensive town plan, which, while satisfying the present needs of a growing population, would also make ample provision for future extensions of the city and secure in his scheme the possibilities for artistic and harmonious development of the town from within.

Hence he summoned his ministers and directed them to resurvey the limits of the ancient city. The temple and the surroundings were again made the starting point of a fresh plan of reconstruction of a new town which as of old grew round

9 இன்புறச் சிறிதி யாண்டாண் டிருந்தவ னிடம்
பெருமற்
பின்புதன் புறப்பு குத்தான் பெருங்குடி
நெருங்கக் கண்டே
(O. T.—Ch. 47-v. 6).

the temple. And with the best available expert advice of his times a plan was prepared taking the temple as the starting point. The plan was drawn up afresh so as to conveniently accommodate the growing population.[10]

Beginning with the right side of the temple, the boundary line was formed along the natural contour, and as the measurement was completed on the left side, it enclosed a large space with the temple in the centre. Hence it was known as Ālavāy, [11] that is, a circular plan, as a serpent would make if it should bring its head and tail together round an object. The full extent of the city was

---

10 இத்தனை மாக்களு மிருக்கத் தக்கதாப்
பத்தனங் காணவிப் பதிக்கண்

(P. T.—Ch. 49-v. 18).

11 வாலினைச் சுந்த ரேசன் வலத்திரு மருங்கு வைத்துக்
கோலமா றுடலை நீள நிமிர்த்தெல்லை குன்றா வாறு
சாலமுன் வலம தாகத் தன்னுடைச் செலவி னாற்சூழ்ந்
தாலவாய் வைத்துக் காட்டிற் றிடத்திரு மருங்கி
னாங்கு

(O. T.—Ch. 47-v. 10).

about nine miles by nine miles.[12] The southern gate was made the great entrance-gate of the city while the smaller gate on the northern side was its exit. Thus the city grew towards the south and had the river Vaikai as a natural boundary on the north. This arrangement of having a big Entrance Gate and a small exit gate was the plan which found general acceptance in all town building in ancient times.

This is after the model of ordinary houses. As was already observed, the word 'Nakar' signifies at once a city as well as a house or a palace. The main entrance of a house known as Vāyil or Grand Entrance (வாயில்) in front, is always bigger than the exit behind which is smaller than the entrance and is known as Puḻai (புழை) (*Cf.* modern usage also புழைக்கடை, literally the small doorway for the garden behind the house).

---

12 ஓசனை யகல நீள முத்தாத் திசைபு றம்பாத்
தேசுடைத் தான தந்தத் திருப்பதிக் கெல்லை
(O. T.—Ch. 47-v. 11).

*The Northern gate and its advantages.*

The city of Madura was thus planned in order to safeguard it against surprise attacks by hostile forces. The invasions into the southern country were always made from the north. As the southern country has experienced several such inroads of invaders from the northern parts of India, the Pandian Kings found it necessary to have only a small gateway on the northern side of the city, as a defence in war.

Further, the northern limits of the city extended up to the river Vaikai. Thus the river afforded a natural defence to the city on the northern side as the enemy had first to cross the river before he invested the northern gate. The local traditions record an interesting story about this exit gate.

Once a Chola King known to history as Kāḍuveṭṭi or the King famed for clearing forests and rearing habitable villages and towns in their place, wished to proceed to Madura on a pilgrimage to the shrine of God Sundarēswara. But when he reached the northern [13] bank of the river Vaikai, he found that the river was in full inundation. And when with very great difficulty he managed to get to its southern side, his progress was further barred by the small guarded gate on the northern wall of the city. And it was only when he explained the object of his visit that he and his retinue were admitted inside the city by widening [14] the northern gate, which was however again restored to its original dimensions as soon as he was escorted on from the city to the northern bank [15] of the river.

---

13 பாங்கடியார் பரவுபுக ழால வாயான் பதம் பணிவான்
முன்னொருகாற் பத்தி மிக்கோன்,
ஓங்குபுகழ்க் காடுவெட்டி யென்றோர் மிக்க வுயர்
தலைவன் வைகைவட தடத்தி னெய்த
(O. T.—Ch. 24-v. 1).

14 கரிபரியோன் றனைநதித்தென் கரையி லேற்றிக் கண்ட
வெயின் முரிவாயாற் கொண்டு புக்கான்
(O. T.—Ch. 24-v. 4).

15 அழைத்தாற் போலப் பொருபுனல்சேர் தடினி வட தடத்தி னேற்றி
(O. T.—Ch. 24-v. 6).

Thus it would appear that when the King planned his city, he took care to provide an adequate defence on the side most exposed to surprise attacks and that he wisely utilised the natural advantage of the river on the northern side.

The walls of the fort were constructed as the natural topography of the land would permit. With the river on one side, mechanical symmetry of the lay-out for the walls would have to be purchased probably at too high a price and with no commensurate advantage either for health or amenity. He did not therefore lay much store by any ideas of exact square, exact circle, a straight line and so on, but he built the walls of the fort in accordance with the environment and the area available. This plan thus necessarily admitted of several deflections and zigzag shape. The city of Madura which was thus encircled by walls which did not answer to mathematical exactness was henceforth called *Tirumuḍangal*[16] or the beautiful city surrounded by zig-zag walls.

This is proof to show that the mathematical accuracy which one might have in a sketch was never sought to be translated in practice in the construction of the walls of this ancient city. The starting point and circumscribing walls having been decided upon, it then became necessary to allot the several classes of the population to definitely marked areas and provide ample open space, public baths, public halls, schools, markets, gymnasia, or public playground, and other appurtenances[17] of the city. The portion for the palace having been duly apportioned, the remaining space was utilised for schools, streets, playgrounds, and separate quarters for the

---

16 மதிற்றிருக்காற்,

பின்னரும் பதியை நல்லோர் பெயர்திரு முடங்க
லென்றார்

(O. T.—Ch. 47-v. 14).

17 வளைமதில் கண்டா ராம மறுகுகோ புரந்த டாகம்
இளரொளி மாடங் கூட மண்டபங் கெருடி மற்றும்

(O. T.—Ch. 47-v. 12)

different classes.[18] And all this was done according to the Śastras (மயனூலின் முறையே) due importance being attached to the provision of groves and parks which were reared afresh[19] in several parts of the newly planned city.

The temple was thus situated just in the centre[20] of the city and shed a halo of sanctity all around. Nor were the streets cut out with mathematical exactness of shape. There were not only big broad straight streets but also crooked streets and small lanes[21] in the new plan. The

---

18 தொல்லை மரபின் மணிமாடங் கூட மஞ்சு தோயி
ஞ்சி
மல்லல் வீதி மடங்கழுக மற்றுந் திருத்தி மாறின்றி
நல்ல குடியும் பல்படையு நயப்ப வியப்ப வீற்றிருந்
தான்
(O. T.—Ch. 53-v. 15).

19 கடிகொள் பூப்பொழி லின்னவும் புதியவாக் கண்டு
(P. T.—verse-2349).

20 நடுவூர் நகர்செய் தடுபவந் துடைக்கும்
அருட்குறி நிறுத்தி யருச்சனை செய்த
(Kall.—v. 14).

21 வீதியுங் கவலையு மிகவளம் புகன்று
(Kall.—v. 44).

broad streets were as wide as a river and the houses on either side rose like tall trees on the banks of the river. The comparison of the broad streets to the bed of a river[22] and of the houses on either side to tall trees growing on the banks of the river, are suggestive of the natural gradient in the streets admitting of a thorough washing down in rain or in flood, and the practice of building houses in towns on elevated ground.

The main entrance [23] gate of the city was as wide as the mouth of the river Vaikai. This is the southern gate referred to above.

The markets were two, a day market where business was transacted during day time generally; and a night market which was open throughout the night. Though these two markets [24] were very

---

22 யாறுகிடந் தன்ன வகனெடுந் தெருவில்

(Mad.—l. 359).

வையை யன்ன வழக்குடை வாயில்

(Mad.—l. 356).

24 ஓவுக்கண் டன்ன விருபெரு நியமத்து

(Mad.—l. 365).

near each other they were yet separate, two big streets having been specially allotted for the purpose. In the day market the business was done in stalls. There was a movable screen in front of the stalls strong enough to serve as a door to the stalls. When the stall was open during day time, this screen was lifted up on a post. It thus served as a sort of canopy in front of the stall. During nights the post [25] by which the screen was held up was raised and the screen fell close to the stall as a sort of door. This simple device combined utility with economy of space.

Small traders and weavers exhibited their wares in the other streets of the city and round the King's palace as well. The streets round the palace where the King's ministers, advisers, and servants lived, were broad enough to admit weavers to stand by and sell their goods. Petty traders were permitted to exhibit the

---

25 *காழ் சாய்த்து .*

*கொடைகவில் நெடுங்கடை யடைத்து*

(Mad.—II. 621-622).

different cloths by the road-side. They spread[26] those cloths on the streets and did business.

The four streets[27] round the King's palace were occupied by the ministers, rich merchants who wished to be secure with their huge treasure, Brahmins, and others, mostly servants of the Royal household. These streets round the palace and other streets, big and small, straight and crooked, were provided with dust receptacles. Such dust receptacles were generally built of bricks plastered over with white lime, and were well maintained at either end of each street. Thus each street was provided with two permanent rubbish receptacles, one for each side of the street. The dust repositories which were thus permanently provided were high[28] receptacles of the rubbish which

---

26 குறியவு நெடியவு மடித்தலுஉ விரித்து

(Mad.—l. 520).

27 நால் வேறு தெருவு

(Mad.—l. 522).

28 உயர் பூரிம விழுத்தெருவு

(Mad.—l. 18).

people threw in. They are known as *poorimam* in Tamil. The adequate provision of such simple and inexpensive poorimams yielded a rich return in health and well-being of the town, by solving the problem of dirt disposal in an effective manner.

The palace and other houses in the city were constructed in accordance with the rules laid down in the Śastras. Architects who knew the rules of town-planning and house-building were employed to survey the surroundings and construct the palace. They take the necessary measurements with the measuring tape, and mark down the lines which should serve as foundation for the building. They take particular care that in the proper adjustment of the palace entrance and the gates, the cardinal points and the deities presiding over such directions are duly respected.[29] The ascertaining of the true position of the cardinal points in the

---

29 நூலறி புலவர் நுண்ணிதிற் கயிறிட்டு
தேஎம் கொண்டு தெய்வம் நோக்கி

(Ne.—ll. 76-77).

construction of a house, palace, or a city was a fundamental principle in house or town-building in olden times.

By such careful planning, the intermediate directions like the North-West and South-East were carefully avoided, so that a healthy and pleasant lay-out may be determined. When all measurements have thus been taken, the architects make the entrance high and wide enough to admit elephants to pass with ease.[30] The entrance would then present the appearance of a wide pass between two high mountains.

A deep ditch was then dug round the walls of the fort and into this ditch was received all the drainage water of the city. The ditch and the walls assured the safety of the citizens against sudden attacks from the outside. Thus to take a bird's eye-view of the ancient city of Madura from the outside, we see first the shady groves,

---

30 வேழம் சென்றுபுக
குன்று குயின்றன்ன ஓங்கு நிலைவாயில்
(Ne—ll. 87—88).

the water channels dug out on the sides for irrigation purposes, and the green fields; [31] and then the deep moat and the walls.

*The rural belt.*

This rural belt round the city was a characteristic feature which gave it a desirable completeness and finish. Where the town ends, the country begins. It marked the natural boundaries of the ancient city and provided for possible development of the suburb in future. The corn-fields and the open roads with avenue trees gave healthy rural advantages to urban areas, and presented a sight at once delightful and refreshing. The rural area provided beautiful surroundings, the city in the midst of open fields presenting the appearance of a central jewel set in emeralds.

And not only from the sanitary point of view but also from the economic and

---

31 புறஞ்சிறைப் பொழிலும் பிறங்குநீர்ப் பண்ணையும்
இறங்கு கதிர்க் கழனியும் புள்ளொழுங் தார்ப்ப
(Sil.—Ch. 14-ll. 1-2).

the social standpoints, this rural area round the city formed an invaluable advantage. To the busy man of the town there was always the attraction of the country side where he could go at pleasure and enjoy the natural scenery and gain that liberal culture which comes of an intimate knowledge of natural things like the flowers, the birds and the streams. And to the peasant, the accessibility to the city would be a welcome relief from the dull tedium of an agricultural life.

On the social side, the town-bred folk would view with due regard and sympathy the dignified vocation of the agriculturist, which has been a theme for the greatest Tamil poets. As the didactic poet Tiruvaḷḷuvar says (Kural 1031), "At several times the cry has been 'Back to the land'[32] and even those who have taken to the other walks of life are staunch on the point. As agriculture is the staple industry of the people and the most

---

32 சுழன்று மேர்ப் பின்ன துலக மதனால்
உழந்தும் உழவே தலை

(Kural—v. 1031).

important of all occupations, it deservedly takes the first rank of all. Agriculture provides the necessary sustenance for everybody employed in other vocations and it is good for meeting almost every need a man may have."

The beginning of the work of tillage, the sowing, the watering, the long struggle with the weeds and other pests, the selection of the manure, the incessant thought about the future, and the patient waiting with an eye of anticipation, and the hearty thanksgiving to God for all His blessings, characteristic of the agricultural pursuit, would be an object-lesson to the town folk, as it would show by concrete methods, the virtues of patience, and resourcefulness, which come from the cultivation of Nature.

These qualities in the agriculturist living on the outskirts of the city tend to elevate him in the estimation of the town folk who begin to regard him. A spirit of common interest and a feeling of neighbourliness are thus engendered on account of such close contact; and this mutual understanding leading to mutual sympathy enhances and develops the social consciousness and amenity of the citizens of the State.

On the economic side, it was a clear advantage to the peasant that he had a ready market in the town close by, for all the produce of his land. This proximity of the town led to intensive cultivation and stimulated agriculture.

When thus the edge of the country comes up to the very walls of the city, the town-bred man is invited for a walk along the road leading out of the city and dignified in its magnificent avenues, and the irrigation canals on either side.[33] And so on, the cities are connected with the villages by such links of open area, fields, and groves.

### *The other Gates.*

The Southern Gate was the Grand Entrance into the city. There was also

---

33 பக்கஞ் சூழ்ந்த நெடுநகர் முன்றில்
கோடகழ்ந் தெடுத்த மறிநீர்க் காலும்

(Kall.—v. 48).

a gate on the eastern side, and a little further from this eastern gate of the city and outside the walls of the fort, there was a spacious garden which was left for the exclusive use[34] of saints and others who were engaged in meditation and prayer. This Eastern gate had a corresponding Western gate from which side the cool breeze played in the streets in that quarter.

*The Forest Growth.*

On either side of the ditch next to the walls of the city there was a small forest growth which was one of the defences of the city, the defence of a newly planted forest. This small forest growth of the newly planted trees, was in the nature of a new garden, which, while serving the purpose of defence, had the other advantage of providing a use for the impure

---

34 அறம்புரி மாந்த ரன்றிச் சேராப்
புறஞ்சிறை மூதூர்

(Sil.—Ch. 13-ll. 191-192).

waters of the city.[35] This device of forming gardens and groves outside the city utilised the drain water of the city considerably. And what would otherwise be a poisonous nuisance was thus practically converted into a useful tract of beauty and delight. The ditch round the city was crossed near the Southern entrance by a bridge. This bridge was constructed by placing over the channel, heavy stones of sufficient length and thickness in order that it may not give way when a troop of elephants pass over it. The gate was also wide enough to admit a number of elephants entering abreast at a time.[36]

Passing the Southern Gate one enters into the city known as Akanakar or the interior city, as distinguished from Puṛanakar or the portion of the city

---

35 இளைசூழ் மிளையொடு வளைவுடன் கிடந்த
விலங்குநீர்ப் பரப்பு

(Sil.—Ch. 14-ll. 62-63).

36 பெருங்கை யானை யினநிரை பெயரும்
சுருங்கை வீதி

(Sil.—Ch. 14-ll. 64-65).

outside the walls of the fort. Here the streets were broad enough to admit the air from the west circulate freely. The full benefit of the cool breezes was thus secured. Here were streets where women of questionable morality were segregated.[37] They were not generally permitted to move beyond these limits into the city. Their streets were close to the walls of the city near the Western Gate. They were allowed the use of separate parks, baths, and gardens specially provided for their amusement and comfort.[38]

The houses in these streets were built according to the rules laid down in the Śāstras dealing with the plan for constructing houses.[39] There was ample provision for light and air, a kind of trellis work

---

37 குடகாற் றெறிந்து கொடிநுடங்கு மறுகிற்
கடைகழி மகளிர்

(Sil.—Ch. 14-ll. 70-71).

38 பொற்கொடி மூதூர்ப் பொழிலாட் டமர்ந்து

(Sil.—Ch. 14-l. 82).

39 நூலோர் சிறப்பின்
முகிரேுய் மாடம்

(Sil.—Ch. 14-ll. 97-98.)

(குறுங்கண்) in the walls providing sufficient ventilation. The courtyards of such houses had a sunny aspect, and the residents sometimes basked in the sunshine in the early morning sitting in such open spaces.[40]

Women of bad repute were always forced to live on the outskirts of the city and were never permitted to mingle with the more honest folk. Women who did not lead a domestic life and preferred to remain unmarried, had a code of morality to which they had to conform. And if they were found lacking in their morals, public opinion was so strong that it censured those who thus deviated from the path of rectitude. Those who have thus fallen in public estimation were publicly disgraced [41] by being taken round the city with a load of seven bricks over

---

40 இளநிலா முன்றிலி னிளவெயி னுகர

(Sil.—Ch 14-l. 103).

41 சுடும ணேற்றி யாங்குஞ் சூழ்போகி
வடுவொடு வாழு மடந்தையர்

(Man.—Ch. 18-ll. 33-34).

their head and banished away to the outskirts of the city.

Musicians, artists, and dancers lived in two spacious streets in this part of the city.[42]

The bazaar streets in this quarter separated the main portion of the city from the houses inhabited by the women above referred to. The streets where merchants exposed their wares for sale were wide and the stalls were located on either side. This was the big market.[43] It was in this big market street that workshops were situated. Palanquins, carts, wheels, axles, conical tops of cars, materials for the chariot, coats of mail, the ornamental elephant's goad, curved bludgeons, shields, soldier's belts, and white chowries were made in these workshops. Braziers and coppersmiths who made brass shields, copper spikes and the like

---

42 எண்ணெண் கலையோ ரிருபெரு வீதியும்

(Sil.—Ch. 14-l. 167).

43 அரசவிழை திருவி னங்காடி வீதியும்

(Sil.—Ch. 14-l. 179).

had their workshops here. And not only the above articles but also saws and other tools fit for carving work in ivory were made in the smaller workshops located along the market street.[44]

Further on from this busy market place where the several workshops were situated, were streets separately set apart, one for merchants dealing in precious stones, and another for traders in gold and gold ornaments. Next were the streets where the cloth merchants lived and sold their goods in the bazaars opened in the streets.[45]

There were again separate streets where food grains, pepper, and arecanut were

---

44 வையமும் பாண்டிலும் மணித்தேர்க் கொடிஞ்சியும்
மெய்புகு கவசமும் வீழ்மணித் தோட்டியும்
அதள்புனை யரணமு மரியா யோகமும்
வளைதரு குழியமும் வால்வெண் கவரியும்
செம்பிற் செய்நவும் கஞ்சத் தொழிலவும்
வம்பின் முடிநவு மாலையிற் புனைநவும்
வேதினத் துப்பவும் கோடுகடை தொழிலவும்.

(Sil.—Ch. 14-168-176).

45 நறுமடி செறிந்த வறுவை வீதியும்

(Sil.—Ch. 14-l. 207).

sold.[46] People were very busy in these streets where the grains were exposed in separate heaps for sale. The food grains thus exposed in the open, were sixteen in number, *viz.*, paddy from grass; varaku and tinai (varieties of millet); śāmai, maize, a hill variety of paddy, ragi, bamboo-sago, gingelly, horse gram, green gram, black gram, beans, Bengal gram, dholl and big beans.[47] These food grains were exposed in the open spaces in front of stalls in order that they may not deteriorate in quality by being kept in ill-ventilated dark rooms. Grain was thus best preserved on the sunny side of the street. And as both for keeping and showing, good light is necessary this arrangement was found very useful and was

---

46 கருங்கறி மூடையொடு
கூலங் குவித்த கூல வீதியும்
(Sil.—Ch. 14 l. 210-211).

47 நெல்லுப் புல்லு வரகு தினை சாமை
இறுங்கு தோரையிராகி எண் கூலம்.
எள்ளுக் கொள்ளுப் பயறுழுந் தவரை
கடலை துவரை மொச்சை யென்றுங்
குடனிலை முதிரைக் கூலத்துணவே.

adopted in all cities. This crowded grain bazaar is a good indication of the localisation of commerce, a cardinal principle in any sound economic town planning.

In the interior were the palace and the streets about it on all sides. Round the palace were four main separate streets where the different castes of people lived; and triangular plots, and quadrangular plots or squares separated these streets from the palace proper.[48]

The plan is thus intelligible. The provision of the main Entrance Gate in the south and the small way cut on the north are the most important aspects of the town plan. On the northern side, the river Vaikai which was sometimes not fordable except by strong boats, [49] provided a natural defence to the city

---

48 பால்வேறு தெரிந்த நால்வேறு தெருவுஞ்
சந்தியுஞ் சதுக்கமு மாவண வீதியு
மன்றமுங் கவலையு மறுகும்
(Sil.—Ch. 14-l. 212-214).

49 மரப்புணை போகித்
தேமலர் நறும்பொழிற் றென்கரை யெய்தி
(Sil.—Ch. 13-l. 179-180)

against inroads from that direction. And as it was obviously impossible to extend the city any further on the northern portion of the city, the main entrance was situated in the south so that it might admit of future extensions. The small gate in the east was rarely used by the busy people. Religious recluses and saints who were engaged in contemplation were here provided with a suitable flower garden, bath, etc. It was here that the disciples of such hermits received religious as well as secular instruction. The ancient schools were in the nature of seminaries where grammar, rhetoric, and theology were chiefly taught. And as the students generally remained with the preceptors under whom they studied, ample provision was made for the accommodation and convenience of the teachers and the pupils in this undisturbed quarter of the city, a quiet retired spot, admirably suited for school purposes.

From this it is clear that it was not intended to provide for further expansion of the city on the eastern side.

If the hermits and religious preceptors were permitted to live in the southern side, they would have to be disturbed when future extensions were contemplated. Under the conditions described above, the city would grow only towards the south, and the hermits and saints would not have to be disturbed. And just as a position in the east was desirable to protect the hermits from the smoke, smell, noise, and disturbance of the city, the King also found it convenient to have his palace erected on the north-eastern side. He would then not only command a good view of the northern-gate, but at the same time be far removed from the din and noise of the busy portions of the city, *viz.*, the southern and the western quarters. Further, the situation of his palace close by the river Vaikai lent it an additional charm and picturesqueness.

Such an arrangement ensured permanent holding and occupation of almost all the houses in the interior even when future extensions were contemplated.

This absence of disturbance engendered a deep love of home, and even the walls of the house which may call up several reminiscences of youth to most people, had not to be shifted in future extensions of the city. The pride of home was thus fostered and hence people improved their ancient homes and grew prosperous. A poet mentions with becoming pride, the old house and the walls as "A decent home with *long old walls.*"[50]

---

50 நெடுஞ்சுவர் நல்லில்

(Pur.—v. 373).

# CHAPTER IV.

## VANJI.

As was already mentioned Vanji or Karūr, was the ancient seat of the Chera Kings. It was a typical fortified city as distinguished from a typical temple city, the conscious creation by a monarch for definite practical purposes. Here also as in Madura, the defence moat, the walls, the streets, the bazaars, and the palace were planned in the same traditional way that has found general acceptance with Indian town planners.

Starting from the outer portion of the city, there were first the residences of soldiers who guarded the city gates. Then the Puṛanakar (Purañcēri) or the part of the city next to the ditch and the walls was set apart for the several classes of people, mostly a mixed population of different social status including the soldiers in the army.

As in other cities so also in Vanji the ditch encircled the walls of the city. The water from the palace, public halls, and private residences fell into this ditch by means of a conduit sluice known as Tūmbu (தூம்பு). The conduit pipe discharged the water of the city into the ditch near the entrance gate where it was covered over with a stone culvert.

By such a drainage system,[1] the water used in private homes for domestic and bathing purposes, was conducted by pipes into the main conduit which poured its contents into the ditch. Those who could afford the expense, had separate baths specially constructed for them in such a manner that water may be filled in or let out of such baths at their pleasure.

---

1 சுருங்கைத் தூம்பின் மனைவளர் தோகையர்
கருங்குழல் கழீஇய கலவை நீரும்
எந்திர வாவியி லிளைஞரு மகளிருந்
தந்தமி லாடிய சாந்துகழி நீரும்

(Man.—Ch. XXVIII-l. 5-8).

When they had finished bathing, they opened the outlet of the baths which emptied the water into the drain which led to the ditch outside.

And not only the large quantity of water[2] used for bathing purposes in the King's palace, but the water used by devotees in washing the sacred feet of saints; the water that oozed out of pots kept in public places where drinking water was supplied to all travellers and pilgrims; and the water spilt by such people who quenched their thirst at those places, were drained into the main conduit in the same way.

Thus while the ditch provided a defence of water to the city it was also a receptacle of all the surplus and waste water of the city. Fish were let into the ditch and

---

2 புவிகா வலன்றன் புண்ணிய நன்னாட்
சிவிறியுங் கொம்புஞ் சிதறுவிரை நீரு
மேலை மாதவர் பாதம் விளக்குஞ்
சீல வுபாசகர் செங்கைநறு நீரும்
அறஞ்செய் மாக்கள் அகின்முதல் புகைத்து
நிறைந்த பந்தற் றசும்புவார் நீரும்

(Man.—Ch. XXVIII-l. 9-14).

water flowers like the lotus (தாமரை), Kuvaḷai (குவளை), Senkaḻunīr (செங்கழுநீர்) and Āmbal (ஆம்பல்) grew in the ditch water and reflected by combination of colours, a beautiful rainbow appearance[3] in the crystal waters. The walls of the fort were high, wide, and massive on the outside. There were several offensive and defensive weapons[4] on the walls of the fort which would throw arrows, stones, missiles, hot oil, molten copper, and molten iron[5] on the approaching enemy.

These walls of the fort were constructed according to the rules laid down in the

---

3 தாமரை குவளை கழுநீர் ஆம்பல்
பூமிசை பரந்து பொறிவண் டார்ப்ப
விந்திர தனுவென விலங்ககழ் உடுத்து

(Man.—Ch. XXVIII-l. 20-22).

4 வந்தெறி பொறிகள் வகைமாண்புடைய
கடிமதில்

(Man.—XXVIII-l. 23-24).

5 வளைவிற் பொறியுங்
கருவிர லூகமுங் கல்லுமிழ் கவணும்
பரிவுறு வெந்நெயும் பாகடு குழிசியும்
காய்பொன் னுலையுங் கல்லிடு கூடையும்

(Sil.—Ch. XV-l.207-216).

Śāstras that they should be high enough so as to be difficult to scale from outside; and that they should have a broad foundation that the enemy may not easily dig them out. It was further laid down that the top of these walls should be sufficiently wide to enable the defending army to walk over the walls and aim against the enemy. The walls should further be constructed of stone and bricks (இட்டிகை) in order that they may not be easily shattered by the opposing forces. As Tiruvaḷḷuvar says in the Kural, such are the characteristics [6] of a good fort, as expounded in the manuals on the subject.

The artistic value of such a fort is worthy of attention. The great element of security in the foundation of the fort walls was made visible to the eye. Then there was the defence created by the trees and shrubs specially planted so as to form an artificial forest. It may be mentioned

---

6 உயர்வகலந் திண்மை யருமையிந் நான்கின்
அமைவரண் என்றுரைக்கும் நூல்
(Kural—v. 743).

in passing that in ancient Tamil literature we find mention made about four[7] kinds of defences to a city, *viz.*, one of land, one of water, one of mountain and one of forest. And where these were not obtained naturally, they were artificially created by the ditch, the walls and the planted forest.

Such forests are known as miḷai (மிளை). People were forbidden to interfere with these trees. Generally, soldiers resided there and guarded the trees which provided a line of defence to the city.

In Vanji also as in other ancient fortified cities there was the ditch, the wall and the forest area.

Passing into the gateway, there were streets[8] where the soldiers who guarded the gates of the city had their residence. It was quite in the fitness of planning, that the guards and sentinels should have their dwellings near the walls of the fort.

---

7 நீரரண், நிலவரண், மலையரண், காட்டரண்

8 கடைகாப் பமைந்த காவ லாளர்
மிடைகொண் டியங்கும் வியன்மலி மறுகும்
(Man.—Ch. XXVIII-l. 29-30).

The distribution of people in quarters according to their occupation gives them the best conditions where they would really flourish. This is a fundamental principle in folk planning, which is an important task of the successful town planner. Passing from the streets where the guards of the fort lived, one comes across parallel rows of streets inhabited by people following different trades and occupations. The order in which the trades were represented in the successive streets was briefly as follows :—Dealers in fish, salt, toddy, cakes (அப்பம், பிட்டு), mutton and ropes, lived in adjacent streets. Next in order were the quarters for the potters, copper-smiths, bell-metal workers, gold-smiths, carpenters, sculptors, artists, leather merchants, florists, astrologers, musicians, chank cutters, pearl bead sellers and professional dancers.

The central market separated these streets represented by the different trades and occupations from the city proper or the urban portion, known as Akanakar (அகநகர்).

On the other side of the central market were quarters in order for the dancing women, weavers, dealers in gold and merchants selling precious stones.

Then came the four streets round the palace intended for the Brahmins, the ministers, the chief military officers and servants of the King's household. The street known as the King street, leading to the main entrance of the palace was spacious and straight.

Behind the palace and the streets, were the quarters set apart for elephant trainers and horse trainers. These people lived in dwellings in broad streets and there was sufficient open ground for them to break the horses for the army, and train elephants which were freshly caught.

The palace was central. And between the palace and the quarters mentioned above, there were separate tanks solely intended for the members of the Royal household. Artificial sand banks with streams running down, parks with flower and fruit trees, fresh water tanks, public halls and rest-houses were constructed about the palace. Thus the palace was within easy reach of the citizens, and yet far from the madding crowd, where the din and turmoil of busy every day life might not disturb the repose of the King.

This arrangement was necessary in order that the same spot may serve at once as a city residence for the ruler where he might give audience to his people; and as a country seat with the necessary appurtenances of bathing places, fresh water tanks, artificial mounds, streams, parks, gardens, platforms under single fruit trees (மன்றம்) and other conveniences, where the ruler may rest his weary head awhile and snatch an hour of calm repose, peace and comfort.

At various places between the several quarters allotted for the trades and occupations, there were public platforms with fruit trees planted over them, where people may sit awhile and chat. This served as a common meeting ground for the young and the old alike. Public halls (பொதியில்) were properly maintained in order that strangers to the city may find free accommodation there. And triangular plots and quadrangular squares were kept as open spaces (சந்தியும் சதுக்கமும்) that they may serve as lungs to the separate quarters of the several classes of the people.

# CHAPTER V.

## CONJEEVERAM.

The great city of Conjeeveram was planned on lines similar to those of Madura and Vanji. Here also there was a deep moat round the city walls and the drainage[1] of the city emptied itself into this moat.

In the outer city were wide open spaces set apart for training elephants and horses for the army. Young recruits to the army received the necessary military training in quarters specially set apart outside the city.[2]

---

1 சுருங்கை நீர்வழக் கறுப்பன பருவராற் றெருகுதி
(Periya-Tir.—v. 25).

2 அரசர்குலப் பெருந்தெருவுந் தெற்றிமுற்றத்
தாயுதங்கள் பயிலும்விய லிடமு யங்கண்
புரசைமதக் கரிகளொடு புரவியேறும் பொற்பு
டைய வீதிகளும்
(Periya—Tir.-v. 100).

There were also on the outskirts of the city special quarters for the elephant trainers, where they made ornaments for the tusks of elephants, cords to hold elephants to the pegs, wheels and flags. Several people who were engaged in making the bow and the mail armour had separate quarters for them in this part of the city.[3]

The planning of the streets followed in general details the same traditional procedure of allotting streets to castes and occupational groups. Brahmins, merchants, agriculturists and others lived in parallel streets[4] and there were four wide main streets[5] round the temple where the servants of the temple lived. The car streets were wide and stately for the

---

3 இம்புரி புரசைகள் இடுகு கூவிர
மம்பொனிற் கலனைகுப் பாய மாதிய
வெம்படை யேனவும் வேறு வேறு செய்
பம்பிய வினைஞர்வா ழிடம்பல் லாயிரம்

(Kanci.—Nak.-v.-22).

4 நால்வகை வருணத் துயர்குடிப் பிறந்த
நல்லவ ரிருக்கை

(Kanci.—Nak.-v. 107).

5 *Vide* footnote (3) on page 21.

chariots to pass easily.[6] The arrangement of streets round a common square and peopled by the several castes was considered very desirable from the social as well as hygienic point of view.

The tanks in the town were surrounded by groves of trees. The lotus and other flowering plants were reared in the tanks.[7]

There were many fruit trees in the gardens of private residences inside the city. The plantain, the mango, and the jack trees [8] known as the three principal fruit trees were mostly cultivated in private gardens. Outside the city there were some fine gardens. The reserved forest (மிளை) was used as a defence to the city.

---

6 திண்டேர் குழித்த குண்டுநெடுந் தெருவு

(Perum.—l. 397).

7 காலுற நிமிர்ந்திடு காமர் சோலையும்
நீலமுங் கமலமு நிறைந்த பொய்கையும்

(Kanda.—N.-v. 30).

8 சித்திரக் கதலிமா வருக்கைத் தீங்கனி
துய்த்திட வரும்பய னுதவுந் தோற்றத்தால்

(Kanda.—N.-v. 36).

The houses in the principal streets were mostly terraced and the ladies[9] enjoyed fresh air on those terrace flats. Red bricks were used in the building of the houses.[10]

When discussing other details of the plan, one finds that while many streets in the city were broad and long, there were at the same time several small lanes and crooked streets also. These small streets were cut out as the contour permitted. They were as important a feature of good town planning as the broad streets and highways magnificent in their avenued spaciousness. The mango trees, and the *mādavi* (குருக்கத்தி) trees were planted at convenient spots along the streets and at the intersection of the streets.[11]

---

9 பொற்களப மாளிகைமேன் முன்றி னின்று
பூங்கழங்கு மணிப்பந்தும் போற்றியாடும்
(Periya—Tir.-v. 94).

10 சுடும ணோங்கிய நெடுநகர்
(Perum.—l. 405).

11 காதல் வீதிவி லக்கே கவலைய
சூத மாதவி யேபுறஞ் சூழ்வன
(Periya—Tir.-v. 106.)

The town planning of this city seems to have been as in other ancient cities a continual growth designed to suit growing demands. It would appear that once upon a time Conjeeveram was stricken with famine and want. There was no rain in the land and all people suffered on account of scarcity of water. Several people left Conjeeveram and settled in the ancient Chera capital of Vanji.[12]

The King who then ruled the land was much concerned at this state of affairs. He was anxious to do everything in his power to alleviate the sufferings of the people. He wished to know why the fair city of Conjeeveram was thus stricken with want and what measures he might profitably adopt to make it more prosperous. He even introspected his own methods of administration to see whether there was anything wanting on his part,

---

12 பொன்னெயிற் காஞ்சி நாடுகெழி னெழுந்து
மன்னுயிர் மடிய மழைவளங் கரத்தலின்
அந்நகர் மாதவர்க் கையமிடுவோர்
இன்மையின் இந்நகர் எய்தினர் காணாய்

(Man.—Ch. XXVIII-l. 156-159).

which had converted a land of plenty into a land of drought and want.[13] As famine was then severe throughout the land, he sought the advice of sages, and requested their advice in the circumstances. He was then advised to open a big tank which could give an unfailing supply of good drinking water even when the monsoon failed, and to plant round the tank an orchard and a flower garden.[14] He acted up to the advice so kindly given and at once set about planting beautiful fruit trees and groves on a site in the south-west [15] of the city and dug a big tank in

---

13 செங்கோல் கோடியோ செய்தவம் பிழைத்தோ
கொங்கவிழ் குழலார் கற்புக் குறைபட்டோ
நலத்தகை நல்லாய் நன்னா டெல்லாம்
அலத்தற் காலை யாகிய தறியேன்

(Man. Ch. XXVIII-l. 188-192).

14 கார்வறங் கூரினு நீர்வறங் கூராது
பொய்கையும் பொழிலும் புனைமினென் றறைந்தத்
தெய்வதம் போயபிற் செய்தி யாமமைத்த இவ்விடம்

(Man.—Ch. XXVIII-l. 200-206).

15 தென்மேற்காகத்
தாதணி பூம்பொழி ருன்சென் றெய்தலும்

(Man.—Ch. XXVIII-l. 175).

the centre. It may be noted that this idea is in accordance with the rules for village planning laid down in the Śāstras that there should be at least two tanks or reservoirs in a city or a village, one of which should be in the south-west (Cf. Essay on Hindu Architecture by Rām Rāz, page 42).

This shows that if at any period in ancient times the country suffered from want and famine, it was usual for the rulers to consult experts how best to alleviate the prevailing distress; and to open parks and tanks which conduce to the health and comfort of the city population.

The foregoing is a very brief account of the history of the town plan of the famous city of Conjeeveram, a city unsurpassed for the magnificence of its broad streets and the beautiful rows of noble avenue trees on either side. The drinking water tanks containing pure water, with the open petals of the lotus and other water flowers reflecting their variegated hue on the transparent bosom of the vast sheet of water, the splendid temples with high pyramidical gopurams which adorn the city and the lofty mansions provided with wide windows for admitting air, and the high chimneys to allow the smoke from the kitchens escape freely, are evidences of the special features of ancient city life and the definite sanitary system obtaining in the past.

Very few places in South India can boast of such an interesting past. As the author of the Kāncipurāṇam has said,[16] "There is not a single poet in this wide land who has not been enchanted by the beauty of the city and of the shrines it contains. All the poets have immortalised themselves by referring in glowing language to the shrine and the city as befits their grandeur and superb excellence."

It is therefore that this ancient city of Conjeeveram with its hoary traditions of

---

16 உவரிசூ ழுலக வைப்பி னுரையமை கேள்வி சான்ற
கவிகளென் றுரைப்போர் தம்முட் காஞ்சியைப்
புகழாரில்லை

(Kanci.—Nak.-v.-125.)

well considered town planning conducive to comfort and working efficiency has extorted the hearty admiration of Professor Geddes whose keen and inimitable perception of things has discovered at a glance the soundness of the ancient town plan of this beautiful city.

The Professor's own view about the wisdom of the plan of the city as conceived by the ancients is very interesting reading, born as it is, of a clear appreciation of the high civic ideals which have animated the architects, who have originally planned the most beautiful city of shrines.

"Here is not simply a city made monumental by great temples and rich and varied by innumerable minor ones; what rejoices me is to find the realization of an exceptionally well-grouped and comprehensive town plan and this upon a scale of spacious dignity, combined with individual and artistic freedom to which I cannot name any equally surviving parallel, whether in India or elsewhere.

"From St. Andrews to Durham, Lincoln to York, Oxford to Salisbury, Bruges to Malines, Aix-la-Chapelle to Cologne and Freiburg, Rouen to Nimes, one finds too readily that contrast of deterioration, even to slum and squalor, which is comparatively absent here."

# CHAPTER. VI.

## KĀVĒRIPPŪMPAṬṬINAM.

Any account of the town planning of the ancient South Indian cities would be incomplete if it did not include a description of the plan of the famous city of Kāvērippūmpaṭṭinam. This city was the capital of the Chola kings until they removed to Uraiyur near Trichinopoly. It is situated at the mouth of the river Kāvēry and is known as the garden city of the Kāvēry, or [1] the beautiful city whose gardens were fertilised by the Kāvēry.

It is also known as Kāvērippūmpaṭṭinam or the beautiful maritime city at the mouth of the Kāvēry. (Paṭṭinam is the

---

1 பூவிரிபடப்பைப் புகார்

(Sil.—Ch. VI-l. 32).

general appellation of towns near the sea-shore. *Cf.* Vizagapatam, Masulipatam, and Cennapatnam, etc.)

The entire extent of the ancient city was ten miles by ten miles. The unit ōśanai (Skr. Yojanam) represents roughly nine miles. In ancient times the ōśanai or nine miles was usually taken as the standard measurement in length for planning a city. For example, we have it on record that the ancient city of Pāṭalīputra was nine miles by 1½ miles in extent. In Tamil the word Kādam represents a measurement of ten miles. This was taken as the unit for planning the city of Kāvērippūmpaṭṭinam which is said to have been a city ten miles square. [2]

It would thus appear that the original design was square in shape. The plan was to have an outer square consisting of gardens and houses; a second square consisting of market places, workshops and so on; and smaller squares towards

---

2 ஊர் நாற்காத வட்டிகை

(Sil.—Page 142).

the centre where the more expensive houses and the palace and other public buildings were located. The site seems to have been selected on account of the fertility of the soil. As Tiruvaḷḷuvar, the great didactic poet in Tamil, has said, "That is a land whose peaceful annals know, nor fierce famine, nor wasting disease, nor ravages of the enemy." [3] The site selected for this city had all the desirable natural advantages, *viz.*, a river, a sea-coast, a safe haven for ships, and general fertility of the land.

The river plain at some distance above its mouth having been selected, the city built near the coast secured safe anchorage for the vessels, and from this safe haven a track was soon beaten to the city on the river itself. [4] Thus the merchandise in the vessels which were anchored in the

---

3 உறுபசியு மோவாப் பிணியுஞ் செறுபகையுஞ்
சேரா தியல்வது நாடு

(Kural—v. 734).

4 தீம்புகார்த் திரை முன்றுறை
தூங்கு நாவாய்

(Pattin.—l. 173-174).

sea was taken in boats along the river into the city. [5]

From the description of the city in ancient classics, we find that the city was broadly divided into two main portions,—Maruvūrpākkam and Paṭṭinappākkam—with a central market between the two divisions. Pākkam signifies a place next to the sea or a mountain. In this case, the word means the village by the side of the sea. (*Cf.* Nungampākkam, Chepauk, and Īnjampākkam near Madras which are villages near the sea-coast and hence retain the appellation of Pākkam).

On the outskirts of Maruvūrpākkam, and near the sea-coast, the Yavanars or Greeks and other merchants from foreign countries had their residence and their place of business. [6] The housing of these foreign merchants near the sea-coast was intended both for convenience and for

---

5 நீர்நாப் பண்ணு நிலத்தின் மேலும்
ஏமாப்ப வினிது துஞ்சி

(Pattin.—l. 194-195).

6 பயனறவறியா யவன ரிருக்கை

(Sil.—Ch. V-l. 10).

the facility of collecting duties from them. Under such conditions the Customs Officers of the State sealed the goods with the State stamp. And the removal of the goods from the docks was not permitted until the duty has been paid.[7]

Petty traders in sandal, toilet powder and other toilet requisites lived in houses built in parallel streets next to the quarters occupied by the Yavanars or foreign merchants. Silk-weavers, cotton-weavers, and embroiderers lived in adjacent streets. The appraisers of sandal, akil, silk, coral, pearls, precious stones and gold ornaments lived in spacious streets next to the streets mentioned above.

---

7 நீரினின்று நிலத்தேறவு
நிலதினின்று நீர்ப்பரப்பவும்
அளந்தறியாப் பல பண்டம்
வரம்பறியாமை வந்தீண்டி
யருங்கடிப் பெருங்காப்பின்
வலியுடை வல்லணங்கினோன்
புலிபொறித்துப் புறம்போக்கி

(Pattin.—l. 129-135).

The grain stalls were located adjacent to those streets and the different grains, pulse, sesamum, etc., were exposed for sale in separate heaps in the open street.[8]

Next to the grain-makret the petty traders in sweetmeats, toddy, fish, oils, salt, betel-leaves, ropes and mutton had their residence combined with their place of business.

The small workshops [9] were located next to these streets. The bell-metal workers, copper-smiths, carpenters, black-smiths, painters, goldsmiths, sculptors, potters, stone-mounters, tailors, dealers in hides, florists, musicians and all other associated groups of people who pursued small trades [10] had their quarters in this part of the city known as Maruvūrpākkam. These manufactories were established as

---

8 வளர்தலை மயங்கிய நனர்தலை மறுகும்

(Sil.—Ch.V-l. 21).

9 Sil.—Ch. V—(l. 12-38).

10 சிறுகுறுங் கைவினைப் பிறவினை யாளரொடு
மறுவின்றி விளங்கும் மருவூர்ப் பாக்கம்

(Sil.—Ch. V-l. 38-39).

near as possible to the outer edge of the town so as to place the labouring portion of the population in the full enjoyment of the open air.

Such an arrangement provided the best physical conditions for the workshops and the homes. Further as the artisans actually lived near the workshops the industrial development would always keep pace with residential development. Under such conditions where the place of business and the homes were so located in adjacent quarters, the workmen were not obliged to go long distances from their homes to attend to their work.

The other portion of the city is Paṭṭinappākkam. The palace of the king was situated in this part of the town and the Raja Street[11] was the main highway here. A few stalls in a bazaar street near the palace vended in the ordinary necessaries. The leading merchants, the pious Brahmans, the thrifty farmers, the ayurvedic physicians, and the astrologers

11 கோவியன் வீதி

(Sil.—Ch. V-l. 40)

lived in separate streets in different types of houses appropriate to each class of people, the various designs presenting by contrast a picturesque sight.

The people who made bangles and rings out of conch-shells, and pearl-bead sellers lived in parallel streets on the western side of the palace. The king's retinue and courtiers lived in broad streets within easy reach of the palace. The Sūtars or those who stand and praise, the Makadars or those who sit and praise, the time-reckoners, and the dancers (சாந்திக் கூத்தர்) lived in various streets near the palace. The cooks, musicians, the drummers in festivals and on the battle-field, and[12] buffoons, lived in houses of various types and dimensions suitable to their calling and circumstance.

Beyond these streets where the servants of the Royal household had their respective quarters, were the residences of those who trained horses and elephants, The open spaces where the horses were

---

12 நகைவே ழம்பரொடு வகைதெரி யிருக்கையும்

(Sil.—Ch. V-l. 53).

trained for military purposes are known as cenḍuveḷi (செண்டுவெளி).

They were circular plots of open ground set apart for the purpose. The charioteers practised the driving of cars drawn by horses in open spaces around the palace. The officers of the infantry had also their quarters here. Thus the king's retinue, his courtiers, and the chief officers of the four divisions of his army —Elephant, cars, cavalry and the infantry—lived in well-built quarters in big streets about[13] the palace. This was the Paṭṭinappākkam or the urban portion of the city. Thus it would appear that in the distribution of folk in distinct quarters in the city, their associations and interests have been chiefly consulted. The aim was to find the right place for each class of people and encourage their dwelling in associated groups in places where they would most usefully flourish. All the outer blocks of buildings were left for bazaars and workshops. These bazaars

13 இருந்துபுறஞ் சுற்றிய பெரும்பா யிருக்கையும்.

(Sil.—Ch. V·l. 56).

served the needs of the respective quarters of the city where they were located.

Between the suburban portion called the Maruvūrpākkam and the urban division known as Paṭṭinappākkam was a large open area where the day market was centrally situated in a site which presented the appearance [14] of a vast plain between two opposing forces.

Thus the central market was situated in a wide open area between the two important divisions of the city. In the market were stalls for selling a variety of goods. Each stall floated a flag bearing the name of the article sold therein. The stumps of freshly cut trees were planted in front of these stalls, that they may afford a cool shade and breeze. The sunshade in front of these stalls was raised on these stumps so that they served the double purpose of serving as supports for the roof in front of the stalls while

14 இருபெரு வேந்தர் முனையிடம் போல
இருபாற் பகுதியி னிடைநில மாகிய
கடைகா லியாத்த மிடைமரச் சோலை

(Sil.—Ch. V-l. 59-61.)

providing fresh air in a busy place. As each stall had thus a tree in front of it the market presented the lively appearence of a park. In the centre of the area set apart for the market and where the main streets intersected, there was a temple dedicated to the Guardian deity of the city. Here was a pleasant square with a tree and shrine. This temple stood just in the centre of the city which was ten miles by ten miles. And the limits of the town either way was ten miles from this central temple. The town plan has been so arranged that this temple occupied a place in the centre [15] of the town taken as a whole.

There was a very wide area of open space near the sea coast where the imports and the exports were kept for sometime. (l. 117. Sil. V.) The goods which had to be taken from the ships to the godowns and the goods which had to be removed from the godowns to the ships

---

15 காதம் நான்கும் கடுங்குர லெடுப்பிப்
பூதம் புடைத்துணும் பூத சதுக்கமும்
(Sil.—Ch. V-l. 133-134).

were kept in this wide area. Officers of the State collected their customs duties while the goods were thus lying here.

Among other open spaces may be mentioned the provision of important parks and tanks specially set apart for the exclusive [16] use of the lame and the decrepit, the deaf and the dumb, the lepers and others who were suffering from contagious diseases. They first bathed in the flowing river Kāvēri and then took a plunge in the mineral baths provided in the public tanks which were efficacious in relieving them of their ailments. After thus bathing twice every day, first in the river and secondly in the tank, they took a walk round the parks. The parks were extensive ones and the walk provided uncontaminated air and good exercise to those who resorted to it.

---

16 கூனுங் குறளும் ஊமுஞ் செவிடும்
அழுகுமெய் யாளரும் முழுகினர் ஆடிப்
பழுதில் காட்சி நன்னிறம் பெற்று
வலஞ்செயாக் கழியு மிலஞ்சி மன்றமும்

(Sil.—Ch. V-l. 118-121)

Public schools (Paṭṭi Maṇḍapam), courts of justice (Pāvai manram), temples to Siva, Subrahmanya, Baladēva, Vishnu and Indra, were constructed at various centres, and the trees and flower plants in the gardens round those places enhanced the beauty of individual temples and of the town as a whole.

The streets were mostly wide and long; but there were also crooked lanes and transverse streets (முடுக்கரும் வீதியும்). As the streets were not narrow, they admitted of the free play [17] of fresh air.

The sea-shore was made beautiful by bowers and pleasant retreats. These bowers were made of the Punnai and Tāḻai trees.[18] Hence the air was laden with the pollen from the sweet smelling flowers of the Punnai (Alexandrian laurel)

---

17 மலைய மாருதந் திரிதரு மறுகு

(Sil.—Ch. V-l. 203).

18 கைதை வேலி நெய்தலங் கானல்

(Sil.—Ch. VI-l. 150).

which kept back the bad odour [19] arising from fish, etc., near the sea-coast. The broad streets, near the sea-shore where the fishermen lived were lined with cocoanut trees on either side.[20]

The main road in the city was that which was cut from the central part of the city to the sea side. This was the sea road or the esplanade [21] by which the imported goods were brought to the stalls in the city. By means of this broad thoroughfare from the sea, the invaluable sea breeze entered the town and added greatly to the comfort and working efficiency of the people.

The chief entrance gate of the city was wide and high. It towered high like a hill,

---

19 கடற்புலவு கடிந்த மடற்பூந் தாழைச்
சிறைசெய் வேலி யகவயி னாங்கோர்
புன்னை நீழல்

(Sil.—Ch. VI-l. 169-171).

20 வாலிணர் மடற்றாழை
வேலாழி வியன்றெருவு

(Pattin.—l. 118-119).

21 மகர வாரி வளந்தந் தோங்கிய
நகர வீதி

(Sil.—Ch. VI-l. 128-129).

with a wide road in front of it presenting the appearance of a river running down the hill. [22] This gate was in line with the main gate of the Palace. In a view of this gate from the outside, attention would first be arrested by the several flowering trees which were planted in a guarded grove next to the city's gate, where the King used to spend some time with his queen to enjoy fresh air and the sweet smell of the flowers.

Thus the parks and the tanks which were reserved [23] for the sole use of the King were situated on one side of the entrance gate. The long road leading out of this entrance gate was planted with trees on either side. This road leading out of the city straight to the bathing ghat in the Kāvēry was a broad

---

22 மலைதலைக் கொண்ட பேரியாறு போலு
முலக விடைகழி

(Sil.—Ch. X-l. 26-27).

23 மலய மாருத மன்னவற் கிறுக்கும்
பன்மல ரடுக்கிய நன்மரப் பந்தர்
இலவந் திகை

(Sil.—Ch. X-l. 29-30).

avenue[24] planted with umbrageous trees. And the citizens who went to the river along this road enjoyed the benefit of the fresh cool air.

The walls of the palace were generally plastered over with white lime and the position of the palace amidst beautiful environments presented an enchanting sight. With the well-kept avenues around, and a variety of trees and flowering plants, the palace rose into view from amid the green foliage of the parks and gardens and was set off to perfection by the shell lime plaster (வெண் சுதை) of its walls.

Elsewhere there were many tanks with high embankments and trees all around, the variegated colours of the flowers of these trees being reflected [25] in the crystal waters below.

---

24 தாழ்பொழி லுடுத்த தண்பதப் பெருவழிக்
காவிரி வாயிற் கடைமுகம்
(Sil.—Ch. X-l. 32-33).

25 உயர் கோட்டத்து
முருகமர்பூ முரண்கிடக்கை
வரியணி சுடர் வான்பொய்கை
(Pattin.—l. 36-38).

As it is necessary that each city should have its own supply of milk, that city which had a plentiful milk supply was considered superior to one where the supply was scanty. It is said that the ancient city of Kāvērippūmpaṭṭinam was self-sufficient with regard to its milk supply.[26]

The ample provision of orchard trees and flowering plants along the sea-coast and near the quarters where fishermen lived, shows the solicitude of the town folk for the health and comfort of the poor. The fruit-yielding trees[27] which were grown in fishermen's quarters are the cocoanut and the plantain. And the beautiful flowering trees Kāntaḷ (காந்தள்) and Punnai removed the bad odour of fish. Further, the cocoanut palms, the tāḷai, and other vegetation are at once useful and beautiful as they tend to bind the

---

26 பாலார் செழுநகர்

(Pattin.—l. 264).

27 கோள் தெங்கின் குலைவாழைக்
கொழுங்காந்தள் மலர்நாகத்துத்
துடிக்குடிஞைக் குடிப்பாக்கம்

(Por.—l. 208-210).

sands in the area. These trees generally flourish in a sandy soil and hence they were selected as being most suitable to grow near the sea-coast.

This in brief is the description of the town plan of the ancient city of Kāvērippūmpaṭṭinam as we find it in the ancient Tamil classic of the Śilappadikāram.

With the river Kāvēry flowing on one side, and the provision of tanks and parks in several parts of the city, the people prospered and trade flourished. This city was therefore marked out as an ideal city. A Tamil poet Kaḍialūr Uruttiraṅkaṇṇinār praises the city in inimitable lines and says,

"I would not for a moment live separate from my beloved, even if the full possession of the most beautiful city of Kāvērippūmpaṭṭinam were offered me."[28]

This shows that the town occupied a very large space in the affections of the people of ancient times.

---

28 முட்டாச் சிறப்பிற் பட்டினம் பெறினும்
வாரிருங் கூந்தல் வயங்கிழை யொழிய
வாரேன் வாழிய நெஞ்சே

(Pattin.—l. 218-220).

## CHAPTER VII.

### SOME TYPICAL HOUSES.

A city like Conjeeveram or Kāvērip-pūmpaṭṭinam which we just described, could not be judged from the outward appearance only. If one wishes to know the ancient city well, he must get to the heart of it. Much of the charm of the city lingers in the houses and in the mansions built by people for their own occupation.

All manner of houses, suited to the tastes and requirements of every class of people are described in the ancient classics. And if we cultivate a familiarity with such houses, we find them quite interesting. They are the products of individual requirements. The house a man has built to live in, is a clear expression of his own personality. And not only in the outward form but also in the details of construction, and in the very atmosphere pervading the house, we find that it bears the touch of individual freedom.

But all of them are built according to the rules laid down in the Śāstras. The houses described in the ancient classics are typical and representative of ancient city life. Exceptional buildings are also described in detail but it has been thought better to confine this chapter to an examination of the chief characteristic houses only. But the examples given here are not exhaustive.

These typical houses were designed by the men who intended to live in them and were therefore so planned and constructed as to be of real use to the occupants. One other noteworthy feature is the material used in the construction of such characteristic homes. Without an exception the material is the product of the environment, and here is a sound principle of economy in the building of a modest, cosy building.

### *The Brahman's house.*

The Brahman required an accommodation where he could chant the Vēda, perform his daily religious rites and teach his disciples. His house was therefore constructed that there was sufficient accommodation for carrying on his routine of work with ease and comfort. There was a separate low roofed cow-house attached to each Brahman house, where the cows and calves were tied to pegs driven in the ground. The bright homes were provided with windows through which the smoke from the sacrificial fire could escape. He kept his house clean by daily smearing the floor with cow-dung. The fowl and the dog were conspicuous by their absence in such dwellings. The parrots loved to stay in such comfortable bright homes and imitated the chanting of the Vēda. The Brahmins lived in Agrahārams which consisted of such houses only.[1]

---

1 செழுங்கன் றியாத்த சிறுதாட் பந்தர்
பைஞ்சேறு மெழுகிய படிவ நன்னகர்
மனையுறை கோழியொடு ஞமலி துன்னாது
வளைவாய்க் கிள்ளை மறைவிளி பயிற்று
மறைகாப் பாள ருறைபதி

(Perum.—l. 297-301).

### *The Agriculturist's house.*

The characteristic feature of the houses of the agriculturists, is the rows of high granaries filled with grain, pulses, and cereals. This is an important element in the economy and house furnishing of an essentially agricultural people. These garners [2] were so high that they had to be reached by ladders. They were old garners, which had been kept on from generation to generation. Grain was stored into them from the top. The cows and calves were accommodated in low-roofed sheds built by the side [3] of the dwelling house. Such houses had open spaces in the front where the children played with toy-carts.[4] The houses of the peasants were modest in

---

2 ஏணி யெய்தா நீணெடு மார்பின்
முகடுதுமித் தடுக்கிய பழம்பல் லுணவிற்
குமரி மூத்த கூடோங்கு நல்லில்

(Perum.—l. 245-247).

3 பகட்டா வீன்ற கொடுநடைக் குழவி
கவைத்தாம்பு தொடுத்த காழூன் றல்குல்

(Perum.—l. 243-244).

4 ஊரா நற்றே ருருட்டிய புதல்வர்

(Perum.—l. 249).

design and shape. They were less spacious than those of the bigger agriculturists, but there was some order in the arrangement of the houses. There were garners [5] in these houses into which were kept the millet and other food stuffs which these poor people stored for a season. Adjoining such modest dwellings was the Koṭṭil or the cow-house where the cow and the oxen of the plough were accommodated. The length of such houses was always greater than the breadth and this was convenient to yoke the oxen and the cows to pegs driven in the ground in a line. When there was no work to do in the fields, the plough, the wheels of carts and the ploughshare [6] were kept in a corner of this shed. The walls of the sheds were smoke-bedimmed as they were also used as kitchens sometimes.

---

5 பிடிக்கணத் தன்ன குதிருடை முன்றில்

(Perum.—l. 186).

6 குறுஞ்சாட் டுருளையொடு கலப்பை சார்த்தி
நெடுஞ்சுவர் பறைந்த புகைசூழ் கொட்டில்

(Perum.—l. 188-189).

The houses and the sheds were roofed [7] over with the dark-coloured straw of the millet which the peasant raised in his fields. These modest dwellings had courtyards or open spaces in the middle where a mortar was fixed in the ground. Here the food grains were husked by the peasant's wife. In a corner of the courtyard the pigs were kept in a small sty [8] improvised by inverting a basket of twigs over them. These huts are witness that simple things are all that are needed in the making of a perfect home.

*The Shepherd's Cottage.*

The houses of the shepherds who had their flock of sheep, were very charmingly built. They were admirably suited to the shepherd's requirements. The pillars [9] of

---

7 கருவை வேய்ந்த கவின்குடிச் சீறூர்

(Perum.—l. 191).

8 புதுவை வேய்ந்த கவிகுடில் முன்றில்

(Perum.—l. 225).

9 குளகரை யாத்த குறுங்காற் குரம்பைச்
செற்றை வாயில் செறிகழிக் கதவிற்
கற்றை வேய்ந்த சழித்தலைச் சாம்பு

(Perum.—l. 147-150).

these houses were short and so the gable of the roof sloped beautifully. Leaves were suspended from these short pillars so that the young lambs may reach them with ease.

Bamboo was used for the rafters and the roof was of the dry straw of the millet. The entrance or gateway was a small one. There was no door but a sort of wicket gate made of bushwood.

The courtyards of the houses were spacious. Small pegs were driven into the ground into the courtyards and the lambs were yoked to long cords fastened to the pegs. The sheep and the goat were let in into an enclosure situated in the centre of the quarters of the shepherds. It was fenced round by brambles cut from the nearest forest.[10] There was always a small forest growth surrounding the shepherd's quarters and this forest was very useful to them. It was not only in the

---

10 நெடுந்தாம்பு தொடுத்த குறுந்தறி முன்றில்
கொடுமுகத் துருவையொடு வெள்ளை சேக்கும்
இடுமுள் வேலி யெருப்படு வரைப்பு

(Perum.—l. 152-154).

nature of a stockade or a defence provided by a thicket of thorny shrubs but was also useful to feed the sheep and the goats.[11]

The common enclosure in the centre of the shepherd's village was known as Erumanṛam, literally the public place of manure. The sheep and the goats which were penned in this manner provided excellent manure for the shepherds. The arrangement of having a central cattle pen ensured a hygienic milk supply to all, while the manure deposited there was also stored and used by the people. This place was held sacred. And hence we find that the shepherd lasses used to arrange religious dances in this pen. The manure of the cattle was thus not wasted but usefully stored and used in common.[12]

*Hunter's Huts.*

The small huts of the hunters who live by the side of the forest were roofed over

---

11 மிளைசூழ் கோவல ரிருக்கை

(Sil.—Ch. XVI-l. 4).

12 கோவலர்தஞ் சிறுமியர்கள்
தாமேரு மன்றத்தாடும்
குரவையோ தகவுடைத்தே

(Sil.—Ch. XVII).

with the leaves of the date palm.[13] In the courtyard of these huts a mortar was placed in which corn was husked. The wood apple tree was also grown in the courtyard. Drinking water was supplied by deep wells in the backyard.[14]

The foresters lived in spacious cottages which had high walls. Their long bows were kept leaning against the high walls of the cottages. They lived in groups in villages which were surrounded by high walls[15] of clay over which grass grew in abundance.

*The Fisherman's Cottage.*

The low-roofed cottages of the fishermen were characteristic. Forest wood and bamboo were used for the rafters and

---

13 ஈத்திலை வேய்ந்த எய்ப்புறக் குரம்பை

(Perum.—l. 88).

14 பார்வை யாத்த பறைத்தாள் விளவின்
நீழல் முன்றில் நிலவுரற் பெய்து
குறுங்கா ழுலக்கை யோச்சி நெடுங்கிணற்று
வல்லூற் றுவரி தோண்டி

(Perum.—l. 95-99).

15 சாபஞ் சாத்திய கணைதுஞ்சு வியனகர்
ஊகம் வேய்ந்த வுயர்நிலை வரைப்பு

(Perum.—l. 121-122).

beams, and the roofing [16] was of the kuśa grass. The fishermen sat in the court-yard with his children and family for his meal. The Paṛi or the basket for catching fish was kept in a corner of the courtyard. The stumps of the Punnai (Alexandrian laurel) tree which grew near the sea-shore, were cut and planted in the courtyards of these huts. The fragrance of the flowers of the tree and the shade of the leaves, made the open front attractive and comfortable. [17] The Indian bottlegourd was a kitchen vegetable which was also reared in a part of the courtyard. During day time[18] the fishing nets would be dried on the white sands. There were

---

16 வேழநிரைத்து வெண்கோடு விரைஇத்
தாழை முடித்துத் தருப்பை வேய்ந்த
குறியிறைக்குரம்பை

(Perum.—l. 263-265).

17 பறியுடை முன்றில்
கொடுங்காற் புன்னைக் கோடுதுமித் தியற்றிய
பைங்காய் தூங்கும் பாய்மணற் பந்தர்
இளையரு முதியருங் கிளையுடன் றுவன்றி

(Perum.—l. 265-268).

18 வலையுணங்கு மணன் முன்றில்

(Pattin.—l. 83).

deep tanks [19] by the side of fishermen's quarters where the young boys angled for fish.

*Huts in the Puṛaccēri.*

The poorer classes of the people who were in the Puṛaccēri or the outskirts of the city, lived in huts roofed over with grass. These modest huts had courtyards where the Indian bottlegourd was reared. When the stem of this creeper is helped on to the roof its leaves form a sort of covering over the roof. This feature is characteristic[20] of such huts of the lower classes of the people. The bottlegourd in the courtyard of the huts of fishermen and of other poorer folk provided a good use for the waste water which otherwise would be insanitary in such small huts. Pigs, dogs and fowls were accommodated

---

19 தோடாழ் குளத்த கோடுகாத் திருக்குங்
கொடுமுடி வலைஞர்
(Perum.—l. 273, 274).

20 பற்றியபைங் கொடிச்சுரைமேற் படர்ந்தபழங்
கூரையுடைப்
புற்குரம்பைச் சிற்றில்பல நிறைந்துளதோர்
புலைப்பாடி
(Periya.—Tnl. v.-6).

in these courtyards.[21] Drinking water was supplied to the whole group from wells formed of earthen[22] rings placed one over another.

*Tope cultivators.*

Another class of people were the tope cultivators. They lived in the groves of cocoanut trees which they cultivated. The owner of each grove had a separate cottage for himself. Its front was beautified by a kitchen garden where turmeric and brinjal plants were planted. The roofing of these cottages was of the plaited leaves of the cocoanut tree.[23] These scattered cottages roofed over with leaves and set in gardens of flowers and fruits, and with a wreath of curling smoke, have suggested to the Tamil Poets, all the excellence of home life, love and quiet.

---

21 வார்பயின்முன் றிலினின்ற
வள்ளுகிர்நாய்த் துள்ளுபறழ்

(Periya.—Tnl. v.-7).

22 உறைக்கிணற்றுப் புறச்சேரி

(Pattin.—l. 76).

23 வண்டோட்டுத் தெங்கின் வாடுமடல் வேய்ந்த
மஞ்சண் முன்றின் மணநாறு படப்பைத்
தண்டலை யுழவர் தனிமனை

(Perum.—l. 353-355).

These small houses of the working classes are very interesting study. Without an exception they bear upon them the distinctive character of the locality not only in the material used but in the very look it has, and in the general details as well.

*Mansions.*

The more expensive buildings are to be found in the big cities like Madura and Kāvērippūmpaṭṭinam. They also bear on them the admirable elements in the mind and the purpose of the several classes of the community who built them for their own occupation and to satisfy their needs and requirements. These big houses were terraced over. And in the open terrace, ladies used to spend some time taking fresh air. The walls were high and were plastered over with white lime.[24] The kitchen was spacious and the smoke found its way through openings in the kitchen.[25]

---

24 வெள்ளி யன்ன விளங்குசுதை நல்லில்

(Ne.—l. 110).

25 குரூஉக்குய்ப்புகை மழைமங்குலிற்
பரந்துதோன்றுவியனகர்

(Mad.—l. 757-758).

The necessity of good ventilation and light was well kept in view. These houses had spacious courtyards which provided ample light and air. There were courtyards in each compartment of the house and also in the kitchen where cooking utensils were cleaned. There were many windows in the walls. The windows were made of a kind of trellis work, the small interstices presenting the appearance of the eyes of the deer or the cow. The expression மான்கண் காலதர் literally deer-like-interstice-air-path clearly indicates the object that was sought to be secured by such a provision. In the bigger mansions, the windows were wider than in the comparatively smaller houses, and many[26] such windows were generally provided. Thus a number of wide windows admitted plenty of light and air to the apartments of the high mansions [27] in a city. In the higher

26 சில்காற் றிசைக்கும் பல்புழை நல்லில்

(Mad.—l. 358).

27 ஆடகச் செய்வினை மாடத் தாங்கட்
சாளரம் பொளித்த கால்போகு பெருவழி

(Man.—Ch. IV-l. 52-53).

stories of the lofty buildings, the windows or the ways for the air were so arranged exactly in the south that the southern zephyr[28] may play without obstruction into the inner apartments. An examination of these lofty mansions and palaces which are described in ancient classics need not detain us further here.

But the simple quiet huts of the other classes of the people and the similar houses grouped together lend a special charm and attractiveness by the method of using the courtyard in each kind of residence to the best possible use of the dwellers within, and without sacrificing in every case any element of the essential physical qualities which a home should have.

## *Roof.*

Moreover the material used for the roofing of cottages and huts is, as was described, in each case, governed by the

---

28 மேனிலை மருங்கின்
வேனிற் பள்ளித் தென்வளி தரூஉம்
நேர்வாய்க் கட்டளை திரியாது

(Ne.—l. 60-62).

class of people inhabiting such residences, their environments and their means. From the ordinary date palm leaves and grass to cocoanut leaves and straw, and from cheap thatch to terrace plastering, there are any variety of characteristic dwellings suited to the needs and the purse of every class of the community from the poorest to the richest.

The houses selected for consideration here, vary considerably in size and accommodation. It is worthy of note however, that all of them were built to suit the requirements of their owners.

As Ruskin says in his lectures on Architecture, "The very soul of the cottage, the essence and meaning of it are in its roof." And in the diversified roofs of grass, straw, thatch, leaves and terrace; and in the courtyards of different sizes in various dwellings used for different purposes and needs, we find that considerations of cost, personal taste, and individual requirements have been steadily kept in view.

The chief general features of the huts, cottages, houses and mansions would appear to be that as a rule considerable attention should be paid to its aspect, and to the securing of the maximum of sunlight and air. The plan is quite straightforward in each case. The most delightful feature about them all is that their exteriors and interiors are in perfect harmony.

It is quite possible to tell from the outside what its interior would be like and how the details would be arranged inside the dwelling. This is due to the most important fact that none of them were built to let for rent but for the actual use of the man who built it.

Such planning of houses is always based on certain fundamental rules handed down by custom and immemorial tradition, and embodied in the rules in the Śāstras.

# CHAPTER VIII.

## RULES FOR THE CONSTRUCTION OF HOUSES.

The general plan of an Indian house may now be briefly described. There are a number of definite rules in the Śāstras on this subject, and they have for their object the securing of the best possible advantages for a residence under certain conditions. These rules enjoin that the ground over which a house is constructed should be carefully examined. It is desirable that the general elevation of the site should gradually rise from the east and the north, towards the west and the south. This position is best calculated to provide ample sunlight and air to the inner apartments of the house. The rules laid down for constructing houses take a comprehensive view at once of the surroundings and of the needs of the people. These rules ensure proper sanitary conditions regarding such questions as the exact location of latrines, cattle sheds, open spaces and so on.

### *Arrangement.*

But the rules are not very stringent. They admit of ready and easy application to actual conditions which may vary from one locality to another. Houses may be set at varying angles according to the size and there is plenty of scope for the pursuit of individual taste. "A place for everything" is the golden rule of the Śāstras and in a site for a building, the following suggestions are given for the proper arrangement of the details of construction. The rubbish may be thrown on the southern side; the straw for cattle may be stored on the south-west; the cattle including the bulls for the plough may be housed in the west; the best situation for the grain granary is on the north-west and the milk cows may be accommodated on the north.

Another plan is to have the kitchen on the north-east; the cattle on the east;

and the safe-room on the south-eastern side of a house.

A third plan which is very much commended in the Śāstras is to have the bath-room on the east; the kitchen on the south-east; the living apartments and the bed-room on the south; the library or the place for keeping one's tools if any on the south-west; the dining hall on the west; the cow-house on the north-west; the granary and the treasure on the north; and the pūja or prayer hall on the north-east. This plan is said to be very conducive to the health of the inmates.

*The Museum.*

In the last plan it is particularly noteworthy that the cattle shed is located some good distance away from the living rooms which are at the other end of the site. Further, a place has been specially allotted for the library which is of great educative value. The library is not merely a collection of books, it is a reading room and a museum combined. In every Indian home there is a modest museum which is exposed to view once in a year. The Navarātri feast in honour of the Goddess of Knowledge is significant. Here in the museum hall, the housewife takes pains to have a collection of valuable dolls, pictures, vessels of brass, copper, silver or gold, and other works of art. Pictures of birds and beasts are also collected and kept. Among other articles to be found in a modest museum in the house, may be mentioned the clay models of fruits, nuts, trees and plants worked in an artistic way and finished with characteristic painting in colour. The different trades and occupations are also represented in the dolls made of clay. The children evince great interest in the collection of specimens for the museum and they collect little pebbles, shells and whatever comes in their own way. When they bring their collection home, the housewife decides if the samples may be kept in the Museum. And it is with very great pleasure that the little folk would hand over the articles to be kept in the Museum. The Museum collection in every home is thus of immense educative value and the insight into the local economic geography of a place which they furnish is very valuable. 'A distinct place for everything' is an ideal in the construction of a house, and hence we find that in the planning of a house a place has been specially allotted for the Museum and the Reading room. But whether a house has all these separate compartments specially set apart or not, even the poorest people would maintain at least one small box containing some Museum articles, which they would treasure with pride and pleasure as a collection worthy of being exhibited at the time of the Navarātri feast under the *ægis* of the Muse of Knowledge, the Goddess Sarasvati, who presides over all the arts and crafts.

The general arrangement foreshadowed in the above three plans clearly indicate the ideas in the minds of the ancients who have enunciated these rules. The principles underlying these ideas are easily understood.

### *Site.*

Great care is necessary in the selection of a proper site for a house. Only such sites are recommended as are selected in accordance with the principles laid down in the rules. The best site is that which slopes to the east, as it would ensure the full benefit of the sunlight. If when a site is being dug out you light upon bones, caves and refuse, that site must be condemned as it is not conducive to health and comfort.

### *Soil.*

The soil on which a house is to be constructed should be carefully selected and tested. A saline soil, a low ground, a water-bound area, a soil where there are cracks and smutty moulds in the earth, a land previously used as a burning ground, an area once used for keeping cattle, a ground whose extent from the east to west is very small, and a land adjacent to which there is a big tank or a lake, are all unsuitable for house building.

The rules further lay down that if the public object to the use of a particular site for building a house thereon, that site should at once be abandoned in favour of a more desirable one. A ground which gives out the smell of oil, blood, fish, corpse or birds, should also be considered unsuitable. These qualities of colour, taste, smell, and touch of soil, should be carefully tested by an expert.

*Position.*

A site may extend from the north to the south or from west to east; if it is situated on the southern side, the entrance to the house should be from the north and if it is situated on the western side the entrance should be from the east. This arrangement would admit free air and bright sunlight to the houses so constructed. But whether a house be situated on the south or on the west, it is desirable that the central hall known as the kūḍam should face preferably the east. The verandahs on all sides of the central courtyard would then complete a plan best fitted to provide light and air to the house. Under other conditions, if a house be situated on the northern side it may have the entrance on the east; and a house situated on the east may have its entrance from the west.

*Material.*

The timber to be used in the construction of a house should be very carefully selected. Wood which fell down in a storm, and wood found in a cremation ground should not be used. The mango tree, the Vēmbu or the neem, the Iluppai (இலுப்பை) and the Vēngai are useful.

*Entrance.*

The entrance should not be on a higher level than the inner apartments. The level of the house should gradually rise from the main entrance. A sloping declivity of the level of the house towards the east is much recommended.[1]

The entrance to a house should thus face one of the four cardinal directions straight. The intermediate directions should be avoided.[2]

---

1 தெரு வாசற்படியுயர்ந்துஉள்வாசற்படி தாழ்ந்திருந்தால் பலன் நீங்கிவிடும்

(M. V. P.).

2 வீட்டில் நுழையும்போது மூலைக்குத்தாகாது.

(M. V. P.).

### *Ethics of House Building.*

The door of the entrance should be fixed on the left hand side of the threshold.[3] And this is a characteristic feature of the building of houses in India as distinguished from the houses in other ancient countries like Greece. We learn that in Greece the doors of houses opened on the streets. Hence when the Greek wished to come out of his house, he used to knock his door from inside as a sort of warning to those going along the street that they may then avoid the bang of the door when it is opened out. But in India, as the doors of houses are fixed in on the left hand side of the threshold, the doors open only inside the house and do not open out into the street. The pials, the corridors and the open space in front of the Indian house are intended to give shelter to strangers who may conveniently stop on the pial for a night without any previous notice, and hence it was desirable

---

3 வாசற்காலுக்கு இடது பக்கத்தில் கதவு வைக்சப் படும்

(M. V. P.).

that such wayfarers should not be disturbed or knocked down by the opening of the door on the outside. Such arrangements of doors, pials, sloping surface on pials to serve as pillows to travellers during nights, corridors, open fronts, and niches or retreats (கபோதகத்தலை) for pigeons[4] and parrots wandering in the air are some of the details of house construction constituting the ethics of house building in India.

*Drainage.*

The waste water of a neighbouring house should never be permitted to enter one's house; it is advisable that such waste water is directed towards the east; it should not go in the south-east or the south-west. The plan of directing such water to go north or in the north-east direction is much commended. The drain water of houses in a row should be let into a main drainage canal. It should not be allowed to remain in any part of the house as it would bring

4 மனையுறை புறவு

on sickness and discomfort.[5] These rules have for their object the securing of the best possible physical conditions for the dwellers in a house.

### *Gateways.*

A house must have gateways on all the four sides—east, south, west and north. This contemplates separate house sites as we find in the west coast. This arrangement is much commended. The provision of doorways in all directions except in the east is least conducive to the health of the inmates. Such a plan where there is no gateway on the east would bring on disease. It does not matter if there be no gateway in the south, provided there are gateways on the three other sides; such a residence is also good. Perhaps the best plan would be to have doorways in all the three directions except in the north or in the west. From the foregoing rules it is seen that an entrance way in the east for the provision of light, and an entrance on the

5 தன் வீட்டில்தானே தண்ணீரிருந்தால் நாசமாம் (M. V. P.).

south for the provision of air, are much recommended as being worthy of adoption in the construction of a house in India, having regard to the climatic conditions obtaining here.

The rules further enjoin that the front, middle and back door of a private dwelling house should be so arranged as to be on the same level and in the same straight line with one another (*Cf.* Essay on Indian Architecture by Rām Rāz, page 46).

*Artistic Side.*

One other fact relating to the building of an Indian house remains to be noticed. The house is generally fashioned after the man. It is considered that the Vāstu Purusha or the spirit presiding over the ground on which buildings are erected, is lying on the ground with his head on the north-east and his feet in the south-west.[6]

He does not change his position. And as he lies in that direction stretching

---

6 வாஸ்து விதான மறிந்து மனைகோல வேண்டும்

(M. V. P.)

himself at ease from the north-east to the south-west, and reclining on his left arm, he faces the east. This position has to be reckoned with, in any plan of a house and the house should be so constructed as to be in conformity with this idea of allowing Vāstu to face the east. This governing idea and the open courtyard obtain for the Indian houses a beautiful sunny aspect which is very important from a sanitary point of view. The entrance door should not be exactly in the middle of the facade but a little to one side.

Thus the dwelling house is constructed on the model of the human body. It must have a doorway and a trellis-work in the wall in the east, and corresponding to the eyes of the man, two niches in the wall one on either side of the doorway, where lamps may be lit. The windows correspond to the nasal cavities (நாசி). The central courtyard is in the nature of a big lung for the house. The entrance gate should be wide and the exit narrow. Thus the Cakravāḷa kōṭṭam, a public place mentioned in the Maṇimēkalai, is described as having a small gateway in the west with a wide entrance in the east. [7]

These aspects of the construction of a house in India have therefore to be carefully considered and kept in the forefront of suggestions for improving present day conditions or for building new homes. For the principle involved is very important. It shows man as an artist with a mind at once analytical and intelligent. The Indian house is an art product of the Indian mind. Man's mind is a part of Nature. And when it works naturally, it works as Nature does.

The entrance, the exit, the windows, the courtyard and finally the insistence of greater length than breadth for a house, all point to the idea that the Indian house is a representation in art of the human body. It would appear that consciously or unconsciously the conception derived from an acquaintance with the fleshy

---

7 திருங்கெதயிற் குடபாற் சிறுபுழை

(Man.—Ch. VI-l. 22).

frame which is the house of the embodied Soul, created by the Great Master Artist, the Creator of the Universe, has been given a form and a visible representation in the construction of a house, a palace, a temple, and a city. Thus the art of constructing a house does no more than carry farther a process that Nature has already begun.

Remembering that Imagination is the source of all art-production, and that the first result of an exercise of the imagination is comparison, it would not be far off the mark to say that the mind of the Indian first worked naturally and instinctively in elaborating his house in an artistic manner fashioned after Nature.

# CHAPTER IX.

## THE MUNṚIL OR OPEN SPACE IN HOUSES.

The distinct characteristic of an Indian house is the open space provided therein. This open space was in ancient days provided in three places in the house, in front, in the centre, and in the kitchen. The word *munṛil* or *il mun* means the front of the house. There was always some open space in front of each house. The central courtyard of houses is even today known as the Muṛṛam (same as munṛil). As originally the munṛil was provided in front of the entrance or vāyil, the present courtyard in houses is also known sometimes as vāyil. Again the word for the bazaar (Kaḍai) shows that bazaars and stalls were originally situated in the front of houses. The semasiology of these words Kaḍai, vāyil or vāśal, and munṛil, thus reveal to us the high antiquity of the governing ideas contained in them.

The munṟil meant primarily an open space in front of the house, *i.e.*, just before the entrance gate. Then the word was applied to the open space in the full view of the gate and this denoted the central courtyard. Afterwards the word connoted any open space in the house and thus the provision of space in the kitchen used for cleaning utensils was also known as muṟṟam (munṟil).

Taking the word *vāyil* (vāśal) we find that it is the *il vāy* or the chief entrance of the house. The open spaces in front and in the centre of the house were thus on either side of the vāyil, and hence their names were associated with the word for the courtyard.

The stall was held outside the house and either in the front open space or on one side of the entrance. It was therefore known as Kaḍai or a place near the entrance gateway. In course of time the term Kaḍai came to be associated more with the stall itself than with the place where the stall was originally located, and hence the word came to signify a bazaar wherever located.

Similarly the word puḻai (புழை) originally meant a small aperture. It was a rule in the construction of the houses that the entrance way should be wide and the exit, narrow. The backdoor way of houses was known as puḻai (புழை) or small way as distinguished from the main entrance (vāyil). The word Kaḍai which originally signified a place next a gateway was then associated with the word for the backdoor and the compound word Puḻaik-kaḍai (புழைக்கடை) meant the backdoor way. This word was later on used to signifiy the entire backyard and garden the sense in which it is now used.

Thus the study of these interesting words from a semasiological point of view gives us a key to the definite principles of house plan formulated in the rules in the treatises and supported by valuable testimony in ancient literature.

In order that the value of the fresh air provided by the open spaces in a house may be enhanced in utility, medicinal herbs and flower creepers used to be cultivated in the courtyards. In the central courtyard in the houses of the Hindus it is usual to plant the Tulasi or the sacred Basil plant on a small platform from one to three feet high, and constructed artistically as a small temple with niches in the four sides for lamps. The garland made of fresh Tulasi leaves is the chief ornament of Vishṇu, the protecting God of the Hindu Trinity, and in worshipping the plant which provides the leaves most pleasing to the Protector, the Hindu worshipped the Protector Himself.

The plant in the central courtyard is watered off and on, but dirty water is never allowed to be poured in. Spitting is entirely forbidden in the courtyard thus dedicated to the service of God. The surroundings should be kept pure and free from rubbish. Water would never be allowed to stagnate even in small depressions in the courtyard where the Basil plant is thus cultivated.

It has been recently discovered that the Tulasi plant commended by the ancient doctors as a medicinal plant of great value is an anti-malarial herb. It has a strong odour at once pleasing and refreshing. The smell of the Basil is thus conducive to the health of the people.

This plant would never be interfered with even by the urchins in a house. A luxuriant growth of the plant in the central courtyard was looked upon as most auspicious to the inmates of a house. The plant is daily worshipped, for the Tulasi is looked upon as a Goddess who brings prosperity to the devotee.

Thus in the worship [1] of the beautiful medicinal plant in the central courtyard and in the use of the leaves of the plant in paying homage to the protecting Deity, the Hindu satisfied his artistic sense while promoting his bodily health also. Thus spirituality and health go hand in hand in such ancient practices which are

---

1 அரசினைத் துளவந் தன்னை யாவினை வந்திப்பார் போல்

(Br.)

ordinarily pooh-poohed as superstitious or otherwise meaningless by those who do not pause to look behind for a motive and an idea.

Towards evenings [2] the ladies of the household would light the lamps in the niches and throw flowers and a small quantity of paddy in the front and in the court-yards and worship the deity presiding over the Tulasi plant.

We have seen that even in the cottages and huts of the foresters, fishermen and other classes of people, there were court-yards and open spaces. In these court-yards also some plant or herb was cultivated whichever is most likely to flourish in the particular locality where the cottage was situated.

We gather that in the court-yards of the houses of the Kuṛavars [3] and hunters,

---

2 பொழுதறிந்து
இரும்புசெய் விளக்கின் ஈர்ந்திரிக் கொளீஇ
நெல்லு மலருந் தூஉய்க்கை தொழுது
(Ne—l. 41-43).

3 கூதளங் கவினிய குளவி முன்றில்
செழுங்கோள் வாழை
(Pur.—v. 168).

the wild jasmine and plantain trees were cultivated.

In other places where the jasmine and the plantain could not be well cultivated, the Nelli tree bearing sweet fruits of high medicinal value were planted. There were sometimes whole fences made entirely of these trees in the open frontage of houses.[4] These afforded a sort of bramble fence much appreciated by the foresters.

Even in the small huts in out-of-the-way places reached by crooked paths overgrown with grass and surrounded by bramble hedges,[5] there were the cotton-plant and the Indian bottle-gourd creeper in the court-yards. These little gardens of verdure and flower shed grace and a ray of hope and delight on such humble cottages.

---

4 மரைபிரித் துண்ட நெல்லி வேலிப்
பரலுடை முன்றில்

(Pur.—v. 170).

5 புன்முசு கவலைய முண்மிடை வேலிப்
பஞ்சி முன்றில் சிற்றில் லாங்கட்
பீரை நாறிய சுரையிவர் மருங்கு

(Pur.—v. 116).

In the low roofed cottages of the Kuṛavars, the Vēngai (வேங்கை) tree was planted in the court-yards and often the Kuṛavars used to dance round this tree in the court-yard. This dance known as Kuravai Koottu, *i. e.*, Kuravai [6] dance undertaken in honour of the presiding Deity of the forest and the copse, who provides sustenance for them. Hence the court-yard is kept clean as the Vēngai tree is considered sacred. In this way the sanitary condition of the central open space of these huts was ensured.

Very often the frontage of bigger houses and mansions were beautified by growing the fragrant red mullai flower creeper over arches [7] made of bamboo twigs. These afforded good breeze and ensured the sanitation of the front of houses.

In the fishermen's quarters near the sea-shore, there were several streets where

---

6 குறியிறைக் குரம்பைக் குறவர் மாக்கள்
வேங்கை முன்றிற் குரவை யயரும்

(Pur.—v. 129).

7 மௌவலிதழ் விரிந்து மணஞ்சூழ் பந்தர்செய்
முன்றில்

(Kall.—v. 81).

toddy and fried fish were sold in particular places. In such places of public resort where liquor was sold, there was a spacious frontage which was kept clean and tidy.[8]

In the courtyards in the centre of fishermen's huts, the śurai or Indian bottle-gourd creeper is planted. The fisherwomen worship[9] the plant and consider it sacred as it gives them vegetables. When thus the plant is invested with a sacred character, the court-yard of sand where it is planted in the cottages near the sea-shore, is kept neat and tidy, and rubbish and dirt are not allowed to accumulate near the precincts. This ensures the necessary sanitation of the fishermen's quarters; and the planting in courtyards of the (புன்னை, தாழை) trees bearing flowers noted for their sweet fragrance, is calculated to give health and strength to fishermen, and increase their general working power and personal efficiency.

---

8 பைங்கொடி நுடங்கும் பலர்புகு வாயில்
செம்பூத் தூய செதுக்குடை முன்றில்
(Perum.—l. 336-338).

9 சினைச்சுறவின் கோடுநட்டு
மனைச்சேர்த்திய வல்லணங்கு (Pattin.—l. 86-87).

# CHAPTER X.

## THE MANṞAM OR THE OPEN SPACE IN VILLAGES AND TOWNS.

If the munṟil was thus the open space in individual houses, the manṟam was the name by which all open spaces in the city or village were generally known. The manṟam (மன்றம்) was originally the name given to a platform and a fruit or flower tree grown over it, in order that the people may go and sit there and have a talk. This platform was generally erected in the centre of a town so as to be easily accessible to all people living in different quarters.

In order to ensure the sanitary condition of this open space, a small or a big temple used to be associated with it. Thus the manṟam also signifies a local temple. The spirit of charity required that people who come from distant parts should be conveniently housed. Hence public halting places or choultries were constructed either by the State or by private citizens in the town. Thus arose a system of endowing public choultries or chattrams for the convenience of travellers. It was usual to construct a chattram on some good locality with ample open space around it. Such a chattram was also known as manṛam.

Frequently, in addition to providing shelter for the pilgrims, the philanthropic rich endowed such chattrams with funds to feed the travellers free. Such public eating places were maintained in good condition and the pilgrims who resorted to such places were received with great hospitality. The poet Kacciappa Śivācāriyār in describing such places in the ancient city of Conjeeverem says[1] that

---

1 அளவில் பற்பகல் தம்மி னுநீங்கியோ ரடுத்த
கிளைஞர் வந் துழி யெதிர்தழீஇ நன்னயங் கிளத்தி
யுள மகிழ்ந்தவர்க் கூட்டியமின் னடிசில்போ
லுறவோ
ரெளிதி னுங்கிட வழங்குமா லோதன விருக்கை
(Kanda.—Nakar-v. 46.)

the pilgrims would be greeted with the same love and regard with which people long separated would be received by their kith and kin. Not only would they be received kindly but their wants would be speedily attended to. They would be fed well and their stay would be made lively and comfortable by kind enquiries and friendly talk.

Thus the manṛam signifies a public hall, a public place of worship, a place of public resort, public walk or maidan, a law court with the Guardian Deity [2] of Justice installed therein, a public bath or a park.

It was usual to plant a fruit yielding tree in such open spaces so that people may take the fruit free and thus satisfy a natural desire to eat fruits. The single tree and seat below (மன்றம்) were provided at various convenient centres in a city.

---

2 அரசுகோல் கோடினு மறங்கூ றவையத்
துரைநூல் கோடி யொருதிறம் பற்றினு
நாவொடு நவிலாது நவைநீ ருகுத்துப்
பாவைநின் றழூஉம் பாவை மன்றமும்
(Sil.—X-I. 135-138).

Ordinarily the banyan tree would be planted in the centre of a village and a big platform would also be raised round it. The birds, especially the fruit taking bats, (பழந்தின்னி வௌவால்) would sit on these trees enjoying the sweet fruit. As the didactic poet Tiruvaḷḷuvar says [3] in his Kuṛal, "the wealth which a person of commendable philanthropic persuasion has obtained, becomes the common property of many people, just as the fruits in the free fruit trees in the centre of villages are intended for the common benefit of all."

The beauty [4] of such gigantic trees with birds of variegated plumage sitting amongst the green leaves and chanting sweet music over them, has been a theme of many a Tamil poet. Such enchanting sights which so much please the adults,

---

3 பயன்மர முள்ளூர்ப் பழுத்தற்றூற் செல்வம்
நயனுடை யான்கட் படின்

(Kural.—v. 216).

4 முன்னூர்ப் பழுனிய கோளி யாலத்துப்
புள்ளார் யாணர்

(Pur.—v. 254).

delight children much more and hence when children gather and play in such open spaces, they are brought up in beautiful natural surroundings most conducive to the healthy growth of body and mind.

The banyan is the tree under whose shade God Śiva, the Destroyer of the Hindu Trinity, suggestively taught to four select devotees the surest means of attaining salvation. This tree is therefore considered a sacred tree. And its luxuriant growth and green foliage render it a source of inspiration and delight. The sight of this noble tree reminds one about its sacred character, that it is the tree under whose shelter God Śiva expounded the great truth of the Upanishads. The attention of the naturalist is arrested by the fund of immense possibilities lying in the tiny seed of the banyan, which sprouts into an umbrageous exogenous [5] tree capable of affording shelter at a

---

5 தேம்படு பனையின் திரள்பழத் தொருவிதை
வானுற வோங்கி வளம்பெற வளரினும்
ஒருவற் கிருக்க நிழலா காதே.
தெள்ளிய வாலின் சிறுபழத் தொருவிதை

time to many kings and their large retinue, in sharp contrast with the comparatively very prodigious seed of the endogenous palmyra which could not afford shelter to even one solitary individual.

To the thinking mind the several aerial roots, which, as they grow stronger and stronger, become firmly planted in the ground and support with their strength the old withered parent tree, forcibly suggest the sacred duty [6] which children owe their parents when the latter grow infirm with age.

The tree which thus appeals at once to the sage, the botanist, the philosopher,

---

தெண்ணீர்க் கயத்துட் சிறுமீன் சினையினு
நுண்ணிதே யாயினு மண்ணல் யானை
அணிதேர் புரவி யாட்பெரும் படையொடு
மன்னர்க் கிருக்க நிழலாகும்மே

(Vet.—v.-16 17).

6 நைந்தடி யற்றவால நடுங்கி வீழ்கின்ற தென்று
வந்த வீழூன்றிவீழா வகைநிலை விளக்குமாபோல்
மைந்தர்கள் தமக்கு நல்லவறிவினுன் மகிழ்ந்துசேர்
ந்து
தந்தையைத்தளரா வண்ணம் தாங்குவர் தவத்தி
னென்றான்

(Ramayanam).

the playing children and the winged denizens of the air, was generally selected to be planted in a prominent place either in the centre of the village or in an open area very near the village.

Perhaps the most noteworthy homage ever paid to this noble tree is that which a poet records in the Tamil classic Cintāmaṇi. He says that the king assigned as a free gift, an extensive area of ground to the banyan tree under whose cool shade he had spent many happy hours of play and jollity while he was a boy. [7] Out of his gratitude to the familiar old tree, he not only gave it a free gift of land but also beautified it by hanging wreaths of flowers over it, and by erecting a spacious platform all around. The open ground was intended to give as wide a space as possible for the luxuriant growth of this

---

7 தான் விளையாடிமே னாளிருந்த தோர் தகை
நல்லாலைத்
தேன் விளையாடு மாலையணிந்து பொற்பீடஞ்
சேர்த்தி
யான் விளையாடு மைந்தூர தன்புறஞ் சேர்த்தினானே
(Cin.—v. 2574).

tree so that people may enjoy the benefit of the pure air and cool shade. The cows grazed under this tree and provided rich milk to the villagers. This shows that it was usual to conserve such areas as public land and maintain them in good sanitary condition to promote the health of the people.

Other advantages accruing from such an arrangement is the natural growth of villages around the area, mostly peopled by shepherds who appreciate good pasturage for their cows very near their habitation. An unfailing supply of good milk would thus be ensured and it would add greatly to the comfort of the people. Again such open areas give space freedom and provide every facility to the young and the old alike for open air pursuits.

The jack fruit tree used to be planted in the public rest-houses [8] where travellers stayed temporarily. The fruits of such trees could freely be used by the travellers

---

8 மன்றப் பலவின் மாச்சினை மந்தி
யிரவலர் நாற்றிய விசிகூடு முழவு

(Pur.—v. 128).

and their children. The kind of fruit tree thus grown in the manṛam or place of public resort was determined by the characteristic fruit trees appropriate to the soil and climate of a particular area. It was considered very desirable to have some kind of fruit tree planted in the courtyard of such public places.

The wood apple tree [9] which yields a delicious fruit which is recommended as a liver tonic and appetiser would be planted in such places that the pilgrims and their children may use them freely.

Again, the Ilandai or the Indian jujube tree, the fruit of which is also good for health, was likewise planted in buildings set apart for pilgrims.[10] The travellers would squat on the floor in the Indian fashion in front of such fruit trees in the resthouse and enjoy a pleasant chat after

---

9 மன்ற விளவின் மனைவீழ் வெள்ளில்

(Pur.—v. 181).

10 இரத்தி நீடிய வகன்றலை மன்றத்துக்
கரப்பி லுள்ளமொடு வேண்டுமொழி பயிற்றி
அமலைக் கொழுஞ்சோ றார்ந்த பாணர்

(Pur.—v. 34).

a hearty meal. These free resthouses which were open to the public were generally very spacious. The space freedom and the presence of fruit trees added to the pleasures of social intercourse amongst the pilgrims who go and stay there for a while. Such fruit trees were planted in public playgrounds also. The children[11] played under the shade of the trees in open grounds. A free and plentiful supply of good fruits was thus ensured to the children. This was most conducive to their health and comfort.

There were other open spaces where Deities were installed in central pillars. The Neem tree[12] used to be planted in such places. The medicinal value of the leaves of the margosa tree is well known, and the pure air which the existence of these trees ensured was of very great

---

11 மதுகை மன்றத்
தலந்தலை யிரத்தி யலங்குபடு நீழற்
கயந்தலைச் சிறாஅர் கணைவிளை யாடும்
(Pur.—v. 325).

12 மன்ற வேம்பின் மாச்சினை வெண்டளிர்
(Pur.—v. 76).

benefit to the devotees who went to such temples of worship. These open spaces with pillars of worship in the centre and neem trees around were also known as manṛam. Children would play about in front of such manṛams.

Outside the larger cities an extensive area was set apart for training elephants and horses. The places where they were so trained are known as செண்டுவெளி (page 88) *i.e.*, the open space where the elephants and horses are walked up and down. Such public training grounds were the distinct features of cities like Woraiyūr where the King's palace was also situated. Near such open training grounds some deep tanks were dug out, where the elephants were bathed. After the bath, the elephants would eat[13] the leaves in the neem trees which were grown all around the extensive open area.

The planting of trees in the centre of villages with platforms around them is a

---

13 மூதூர் வாயிற் பனிக்கய மண்ணி
மன்ற வேம்பின் ஒண்குழை மலைந்து

(Pur.—v. 79).

characteristic feature of several Indian villages which take their names after the trees which are grown in them. And even to-day one finds such platforms and trees in many villages.

It is considered an act of virtue to plant the *araśu* (Ficus Religiosa) and the neem tree together in a certain open space preferably on the banks of a running river or a stream, or on the bund of a tank, and to erect a platform around and install a deity under the tree.

The vestiges of this good old ideal are even to-day to be seen in the platforms and trees in several villages and towns in the Madras Presidency. In Māyavaram there is now a locality known as Māvaḍi mēḍai or the platform round the foot of the mango tree. These shady platforms afford space for children to gather and play. People resort to such clean spots rendered useful and beautiful by the fruit tree growing there.

The square in the centre of the quarters occupied by shepherds has elsewhere been described. It is known as "eru manṛam" or the open space for keeping cattle and collecting manure. We are told that people would sit in such places and enjoy[14] the time honoured sports such as cock-fights, goat-fights and so on.

The maintenance of bathing tanks, the construction of river ghats, the provision of public squares, the building of rest-houses, the planting of fruit trees, and the erection of platforms around them were always suggested as acts of virtue in which people should take an abiding interest.

The central tree and the platform were thus quite a common feature of all ancient cities and villages in South India.

Any fruit tree was better than no tree at all. And though the palmyra[15] tree could not give much shelter, still in places where the soil was most favourable

---

14 மலர்தலை மன்றத்துப் பலருடன் குழீஇ
மேழகத் தகரொடு சிவல் விளையாட

(Pattin.—l. 69-77).

15 நடுவூருள் வேதிகை சுற்றுக்கோட் புக்க
படுபனை யன்னர் பலர்நச்ச வாழ்வர்.

(Nal.—v. 96)

only to its growth, it was planted in the centre of such villages and a platform was also constructed around. The village folk ate those fruits freely and spent some time in the open area round the tree.

Such open spaces and dilapidated old temples with trees growing near them were resorted to by the grey haired[16] old folk also who spent their time mostly in playing at dice sitting in those open *manṛams*.

---

16 பலிகண் மாறிய பாழ்படு பொதியில்
நரைமூ தாளர் நாயிடக் குழிந்த
வல்லி னல்லகம்.

(Pur.—v. 52).

View of a Street in a Garden Village.

General view of the Tank in the centre of a Garden Village.

# CHAPTER XI.

## THE GARDEN VILLAGE.

When a village or a town is intimately associated with a central temple, such a sacred association makes the village or the town a garden area in the best sense of the term. It is a well known fact that every shrine is sanctified by a combination of three elements Stala, Tīrtha, and Mūrty, *i.e.*, the soil, the water and the deity. Of these the Stala Vṛksha or the tree sacred to the locality on account of its association with the temple is a very important factor.

There could be no place of worship without an appropriate tree or plant growing near it and associated with it. To enumerate the different fruit trees, flowering plants and other variety of creepers with which every shrine in South India is associated, would be beyond the scope of this work. It would be an interesting enquiry by itself. The principle underlying the cultivation of trees and plants in such shrines of great antiquity is clearly intelligible. Such ideals have for their object the promotion of healthy conditions of living.

If in a certain area, a particular tree was considered sacred on account of its association with the temple, that tree or plant would naturally find favour with other private citizens also, who would cultivate such trees in their own private gardens and in the public parks as well. Thus arose a system of rearing flower gardens, orchard gardens and avenue trees which yielded a rich return in the health of the community.

Trees, plants, shrubs, creepers and bushes grow in places most suitable to their growth and such natural conditions as the inter-relation between a given soil and its vegetation was availed of to the greatest advantage in the building of temples in South India.

On account of such temples, small and big, studded throughout the land, and by means of the sanitary conditions which they promoted, a healthy stimulus was given to private effort in such direction as the cultivation of a flower garden. It is generally held that the founding of gardens is an act of virtue most pleasing to the Gods. Health problems were thus approached from the side of religion.

As the Tēvāram or the garland of religious verses says, [1] "A place without a temple is an arid waste." That is to say, such a locality is considered uninhabitable.

The impetus given through the medium of religion to the construction of temples and the opening of tanks, gardens and the like, has been responsible for the existence to-day in South India of temples in almost every village.

These temples are of any variety in importance and construction. Many of

---

1 திருக்கோயிலில்லாத திருவிலூர்
ஊரல்ல அடவிகாடே

(Tev.).

them are old temples with imposing gateways, tanks and gardens. Some are new and comparatively smaller than the older ones which are described in the ancient Stala Purāṇās and in the religious verses sung in olden times. The bigger temples are those of Śiva and Vishṇu. The other deities have also temples built in their honour throughout the Dekkan. But of whatever kind they may be, they are important in this way that they are of considerable benefit to the public health of a locality. For here it is that the existing natural features such as ponds, tanks, springs, rivers, village greens, groves, trees, etc., are used to their best advantage in making the village look as picturesque as possible. The towers of a temple may not be very high or the local feasts most imposing. But so long as there is a temple, it adds amenity to the otherwise dull and eventless life in a village.

The temple may be ever so modest a structure, but it must have a tank adjoining it ; and also a flower garden and an open space about it. And the practice of building houses abutting round such an open square or in front of the tank adjoining the temple is very useful from a hygienic point of view, for admitting fresh air and light to each and every home.

Thus came into existence a number of villages each with a central temple and a tank and a garden adjoining it. Streets were then formed round the temples and houses were built for the use of those temple servants to whom it was an advantage to live near their place of work. And likewise, rows of houses grew in a well ordered plan on all sides of the tank. And as fresh temples were constructed, villages grew in the same manner on the model of the older villages. And so on, villages and cities with temples and public baths were studded throughout the length and breadth of the Southern country.

And just as fruit trees or other plants were cultivated in the temple garden, so in private homes also people planted the same kind of trees as are found in the local temple. Thus the central tree, the temple plant, the private gardens, and the avenue trees gave a village its garden character thereby and promoted health conditions for the inhabitants. This is the idea which has been actually translated into active practice in most of the South Indian villages.

Of these villages in South India, the older ones are those which contain ancient shrines. And it is noteworthy that every such shrine of high antiquity and wealth of tradition is always associated with a fruit tree or flower plant or some kind of herb or shrub.

The names of several villages are thus derived from the names of such characteristic natural features as trees, plants, river side and so on.

We may now consider a few villages and towns with shrines with a view to appreciate the character of the sites from the point of view of the town planner. To begin with, we may take Māyavaram in the Tanjore District which contains a famous shrine. And as the mango tree is sacred on account of its association with the shrine, the popular idea of cultivating the tree in other places in the village has found ample support and practice in the single tree and platform round the magnificent mango tree, the Māvaḍi mēḍai already described. The mango tree is the sacred tree associated with the Śiva temple in Conjeevaram also.

The Ilandai or the Indian Jujube (இலந்தை) is a fruit bearing tree, whose fruits are good for health. This tree is found in the shrines in the villages of Tiruviḷambūr (Chingleput District); Kīḻvēḷūr and Ilanduṛai (Tanjore District).

The cocoanut tree is very widely grown in several places notably in the shrine of Āḍuturai.

It is clear that such fruit trees were planted in shrines and villages in order that people may take them free whenever they wanted them.

In a Stala Purāṇa or local tradition connected with a temple where the sacred tree is the cocoanut palm, we gather that the tender cocoanut was once very useful to a lady who fainted away with thirst as water could not be had anywhere near.

The palmyra is the fruit tree in the old temples at Tiruppanandāḷ and Tiruppanaiyūr (Tanjore District), Panankāṭṭūr (Chingleput District), Puṛavār Panankāṭṭūr and Panayavaram (South Arcot District).

The white Nāval or Jambu is the fruit tree in the famous shrine of Tiruvānaikkā near Trichinopoly. This noble fruit tree is well maintained here even to-day and is separately worshipped. The black nāval is the fruit tree in Tirunāvalūr.

Of flower creepers, the mullai which bears a variety of jasmine is associated with the shrines in Śikkil and Tirukkarukāvūr (Tanjore District), Tirumullaivāyil (Chingleput District). The Pādiri or the trumpet-flower tree is the sacred tree in the shrine of Tiruppādirippuliyūr (South Arcot Dt.). The flower has a beautiful violet hue and a subdued fragrance at once sweet and pleasing. It is usual to place a few flowers of the Pādiri tree in a fresh pot before storing water in it. [2] The flower lends a fragrance to the pot which in its turn adds a delicious aroma and cool quality to the drinking water so stored. This practice of cooling the water by means of such flowers is quite common. Hence this tree is often cultivated on the bunds of tanks supplying drinking water to the people. The old shrine of Avanāśi (Coimbatore District) is associated with this noble tree.

The Punnai or Alexandrian laurel which bears a sweet scented flower is the tree cultivated in the shrines at Mylapore (Madras), Tiruppukalūr (Tanjore District), Sankaranaināṛ Koil (Tinnevelly District).

In the shrines in the villages in Tiruvalaṅkāḍu and Tirukkaccūr (Chingleput District) and Tiruvalāmpoḻil (Tanjore District), the banyan tree which affords delightful shelter on account of its extensive canopy of green foliage, is cultivated and maintained as a sacred tree associated with the temples.

---

2 ஒண்ணிறப் பாதிரிப்பூப் புத்தோடு சேர்தலால்
தண்ணீர்க்குத் தான்பயந் தாங்கு (Nal.—v. 139).

In other shrines, trees of medicinal value are sometimes cultivated and the surrounding air is made pure and healthy thereby. The *nelli* tree which gives the nelli fruit, which is recommended as a liver tonic, is the sacred tree in the shrine in a village which takes its name after the tree and is known as Tiru nellikkā literally the beautiful nelli grove village.

The *punka* tree is the sacred tree in the shrine at Tirupunkūr (Tanjore District) and the neem tree in Vēmbattūr (Tanjore District).

Again the Indian gall-nut is the tree grown in the garden in the shrine at Tirukkuṛukkai near Māyavaram and the tānṛi (Terminalia Bellerica) whose fruit has a quantity of tannin in it, is the sacred tree in Kāḷahasti.

The parāy is a plant whose bark has curative properties in eczema and similar complaints. This is the sacred plant in a village which takes its name after the chief plant in the temple and is known as Tirupparāyttuṛai (Trichinopoly District).

The leaves of the medicinal plant Viḻuti (Cleome fruticosa) act as a mild purgative. This medicinal plant is the sacred plant in the shrine at Tiru vīḻi miḻalai (Tanjore District).

The vilva tree (Crataeva religiosa) which produces the vilva fruit having good medicinal property, is associated with the old shrine at Villianūr (near Pondicherry). The village is known as Vilvāraṇyam or the vilva forest. The purāṇa states that it was once a forest of vilva trees. The vilva plant is also cultivated in the temple at Tirukkoḻḻamputtūr (Tanjore District).

These facts go to show that in the building of shrines and in the planning of villages round them, all these natural features of a locality as the plant or a tree growing there, have been utilised to the greatest advantage. By such simple device of developing the characteristic points of a village vegetation, the health and happiness of the people have been ensured, while the beauty of the village was enhanced all the more by the orderly development of such pronounced natural features. That this is so may be seen in the importance attached to the Kuśa grass, in Tirunaḷḷār (Tanjore District); the Kaḷa (களா) (Carissa diffusa) in Pāpanāśam; the Virai, a flowering shrub, in Viraimānakar near Śākkōṭṭai (Tanjore District); the old tamarind tree in Āḻwār Tirunakari; the Kaḷḷi (கள்ளி or milk hedge or Indian tree spurge) plant in Tirukkaḷḷil near Conjeeveram; and the Viḻal (Cuscus grass) in the shrine at Tiruviḷa nakar, east of Māyavaram. It may be mentioned that the root of this Viḻal is sometimes kept in drinking water; the root adds a sweet aroma to the water and cools it.

It is easy to quote several instances where the garden and orchard have been given much prominence in the rearing of villages. It is an interesting study in the onomatology of South Indian villages and shrines that the village takes its name after a tree or a plant or a river close by. To take a few examples by way of illustration in a field which offers wide scope for a very interesting study in the

Economic Geography of South India, the suffix poḷil in place names like Tiruvālam poḷil suggest a grove; the suffix tōṭṭam signifies the presence of a spacious garden, as Pūntōṭṭam and Peruntōṭṭam (Tanjore District).

Similarly tuṛai signifies a place near a river or a tank, *e.g.*, Tirupperuntuṛai and Tiruvāvaḍutuṛai take their names after the sacred water near. Ulavāūrṇi (Tanjore District) takes its name after the central tank. The name means literally the village with a tank which never fails.

There are innumerable instances of villages being named after a tree or a plant which arise and flourish on account of the natural conditions of vegetation characteristic of a locality. For, as we saw, Tiruppātirippuliyūr (Cuddalore New Town) takes its name after the Pādiri tree in the temple. Villianūr is named after the Vilva forest in which it is situated, and so on in the case of many other villages and towns.

And when new villages or towns are built up, it is natural to adopt such old names which have a fascination over the mind of the people and hence these old names are adapted in naming the new villages. The temples and other conditions are also likewise adapted on the model of the old villages. It is to this wholesome practice of imitating ancient idealism and practice in modern conditions that we owe the existence to-day of more than one village bearing the same name.

Another important feature connected with the cultivation of such plants and trees in village shrines is the medicinal value attached to the water iu the temple tank. The water in such tanks is rendered valuable on account of the medicinal properties of the plant or tree growing about the tank. This accounts for the marvellous cures of diseases said to have been wrought in ancient times by using the water in the tanks of such temples for bathing and drinking. Moreover the flowers and leaves of the sacred trees growing in and around a temple are used in the daily offering to the deity in the temple. The clean water used in the temples washes away these flowers and this water is drained into the temple tank. The water in the tank thus gets the properties and medicinal value of the trees and herbs in the locality.

Thus the idea of garden and orchard have always played a very important part in the building up of villages and shrines. And the town planning movement of to-day must seek to restore all the healthy elements and commendable aspects of the old village life vouchsafed by such æsthetic and hygienic conditions conceived by the ancients as contributing to the health and well-being of the villagers.

As illustrating the above principles one might take the case of Tirukkaḻuk-kunṛam, a favourite health resort in the Chingleput District. This village owes its importance to a big tank created by ancient foresight, labour, and sacrifice, and adjoining a hill overgrown with herbs and plants. The principal shrine is situated on the top of this hill. The person who goes to this health resort takes a plunge into the cool waters of the tank and goes round the hill enjoying the pure fresh air which blows from the hill. The circuit around the hill is about two miles and two furlongs. And the invigoration of body and mind which goes with the bath and the subsequent walk round the sacred hill promote the health of the people. Moreover, the entire village presents the appearance of a garden village with its fields, avenue trees, groves and flower gardens. The water in the tank derives its essential medicinal property by its association with the medicinal herbs and plants which grow profusely on the hill and are not cut or otherwise interfered with. The natural run of rain water which falls on the hill is directed to the tank by a channel which has been well thought out and carefully planned. Thus the hill and the tank are protected by the sanctity associated with the temple and its surroundings, and hence yield a valuable return in health and amenity.

We have already indicated that it is usual to cultivate fruit trees in the gardens of houses. The trees thus cultivated are the plantain, the jack, the cocoanut, and the mango.[3] Such private gardens are in a very special sense characteristic. These individual gardens of the houses and cottages reflect the spirit of the garden village. They show the supreme importance attached by the common folk to fruit trees and other plants which yield a rich return in beauty, health, and wealth. And not only in the small gardens of individual houses but also on the outskirts [4] of cities and villages, flower gardens were specially reared. We learn that ladies would go to these gardens to gather flowers.

The cocoanut [5] trees were ordinarily planted in the fields and roads in order

---

3 தேம்பழுத் தினியநீர் மூன்றுந் தீம்பலா
மேம்பழுத் தளிந்தன சுளையும் வேரியும்
மாம்பழக் கனிகளு மதுத்தண் டட்டமும்
தாம்பழுத் துளசில தவள மாடமே

(Cl.—N-v. 14.)

4 மணிமேகலைதான் மாமலர் கொய்ய
அணிமலர்ப் பூம்பொழி லகவயிற் சென்றதும்

(Man.—Padikam. l. 38-39).

5 தெங்கின் இளநீ ருதிர்க்கும் வளமிகு நன்னாடு

(Pur.—v. 29).

that people may use the nuts freely. The cocoanut and the palmyra trees were commonly cultivated in the fields on either side of the roads and in private gardens as well. Little urchins [6] ate the cocoanuts and the palmyra fruit to their heart's content. It is said that little children go up the strawstacks piled up in the fields and easily reach the palmyra fruits.

The black nāval trees bearing edible fruits were planted on either side of a river for people to eat the fruits as they liked. The river banks [7] thus presented a length of landscape beauty and fruitfulness. And both from the standpoint of beauty and of utility the fruit trees conduced to public health.

---

6 வன்கை வினைஞர் புன்றலைச் சிறாஅர்
தெங்குபடு வியன்பழ முனையிற் றந்தையர்
குறைக்கண் ணெடும்போர் ஏறி விசைத்தெழுந்து
செழுங்கோட் பெண்ணைப் பழந்தொட முயலும்

(Pur.—v. 61).

7 நல்யாற் றெக்க ரேறி
கருங்கனி நாவ லிருந்துகொய் துண்ணும்

(Pur.—v. 177).

Even the small gardens by the side of the cottages where the poor folk lived were beautified by flower trees like the Pādiri, and the women decorated [8] their heads with garlands of such flowers. These poor women-folk were always animated by an inborn instinct to maintain a fruit or flower tree in their tiny gardens. Such poor folk always enjoyed the use of a small garden close by their huts. The gardens were located by the side [9] of the houses and were generally used as kitchen gardens to cultivate greens and other vegetables for daily consumption. This suggests that there were spaces between the huts.

Those who could afford a large area for a garden and the necessary conveniences, cultivated the beautiful Punnai [10] flower

---

8 கைவள் ளீகைப் பாணன் சிறுகுடி
பாதிரி கமழு மோதி யொண்ணுதல்
(Pur.—v. 20).

9 வளைக்கை விறலியர் படப்பைக் கொய்த
வடகு
(Pur.—v. 140).

10 நறவங்கொப் புளித்தலி ஞெகுபுன்னை பூத்தன
(Cin.—v. 74).

tree in their gardens. Likewise, where conditions were favourable, arecanut[11] palm trees and betel leaf creepers were grown in the gardens of houses.

On account of their utility and beauty the cocoanut trees used to be planted as avenue[12] trees on either side of the streets of a city. Avenue trees were planted in all the important roads[13] leading into the cities.

It was the ambition of town builders to have their towns planned in such a manner that they may be ideal garden cities. Thus the village known as Kiḍangil now near Tindivanam, South Arcot District, was once in the occupation of a chief who is styled as the chief of the

---

11 பாளைமென் கமுகின்பழமெல்லிலை
நீளவெண்மாடத்து

(Cin.—v. 132).

12 தெங்கி னொண்பழத் தெள்ளமு தத்தினற்
பங்க மெய்தி மறுகின் பரப்பெலாம்

(N.—Nak.—v. 26).

13 வீயா யாணர் வளங்கெழு பாக்கத்துப்
பன்மரம் நீளிடைப் போகி

(Perum.—l. 377-368).

"Garden city of Kiḍangil."[14] Special emphasis is laid upon the garden in the very name and plan of this old town.

The inborn instinct in man to appreciate gardens and flowers was further fostered and strengthened by religious ideals. To destroy parks and gardens was considered as heinous a crime[15] as murder, infanticide, etc. The best way to please God is to cultivate a flower garden which would provide fresh fragrant flowers for the daily offering in temples.[16] It is also enjoined by religion that fruit trees should be planted wherever possible. Ideals of life enjoined by suggestions of religion have been specially useful in a land, where religion and sanitation are, from time immemorial, most intimately associated. In

14 கிளைமலர்ப் படப்பைக் கிடங்கிற் கோமான்
(Sir.—l. 160).

15 ஆராமங்கள ழித்தோருமத்தி பெருந்தவன்யிரோரும்
(Br.).

16 காவினையிட்டுங் குளம்பல தொட்டுங் கனிமனத்
தால்
பூவினைக்கொய்து மலரடி போற்றுதும்
(Tev.—I).

India, health problems have been generally approached from the side of religion. This provided the motive power for people to take a deep interest in tanks, gardens, parks, avenues and so on, which promote the general health of the community.

# CHAPTER XII.

## A RETROSPECT.

We may now consider in a general way certain facts with reference to the methods pursued by the ancients when planning towns and villages. Some important suggestions may be obtained in this manner by searching back in literary works that are now the classics of the past, for those first principles which underlie the ancient art of town planning.

There is a marked uniformity in methods in the planning of Indian cities, new towns being generally planned on the lines of the old cities. According to tradition the extent of a city was preferably nine miles each way or at least in length. The city is divided generally into three portions, *viz.*, the outer, the intermediate and the central. And each part has its own parks, tanks, public spaces and streets. Such a division is important for the proper distribution of castes, trades and occupational groups. Taking the outer city, there are first the wide open areas where horses and elephants are trained. The artifical forests, the ditch and the fort are then planned for the entire city. These features enclose an extensive area, and open spaces, residential quarters and streets are planned with due regard to the extent taken up and other subsequent improvements and extensions that may afterwards come in.

The elephant trainers, [1] horse trainers, and the soldiers lived in the outer city. They lived in long straight streets and made ivory ornaments and furniture.

The chariot drivers [2] also had their residence in this part of the city. They lived in separate streets and taught

1 முத்துடைவெண் மருப்பீர்ந்து &c.

(Cin.—v.-83).

2 இடு தேர்ச்சாரிகை......&c.

(Cin.—v.-84).

soldiers the art of driving chariots in war. Likewise there was another open space planned in the form of a circle which was used as a race course. Among other features in the city may be mentioned the open spaces, where the soldiers of the infantry practised swordsmanship and archery.

In the intermediate portion of the city, were broad streets where the merchants and traders lived.

In the central portion or akanakar was situated the palace of the king. Separate baths were improvised here for the exclusive use of the Queen and other ladies of the Royal household. Some of these baths were artificial reservoirs of water which could be filled and emptied at will. There were also artificial [3] mounds of stone and sand where the members of the Royal family would spend some time.

The parks by the side of the palace contained deer and other games. Such parks were guarded by soldiers and were

3 எந்திரக் கிணறுமிடுங்கற் குன்றமும்

(Man.—Ch. XIX.-l. 101).

closed to the public.[4] There were other tanks and flower gardens [5] which were also reserved for the exclusive use of the Queen and other princesses. Platforms (தெற்றி) were raised at convenient places in these parks and gardens. In making arrangements for the amenities of the Royal household, the kings combined usefulness with beauty and taste. One of such artificial features planned near the palace in ancient times, is the Samudram, a beautiful sheet of water near Tanjore, said to have been dug out to give an idea of the ocean to the ladies of the Royal family. This circumstance had the advantage of combining utility with a pleasant feature of town planning.

*Streets.*

The streets in the central city were mainly the car-streets (தேர்செல்வீதி) and the Rajah streets (ராஜப்பெருந்தெரு) which

---

4 உய்யா னத்திடை யுணர்ந்தோர் செல்லார்

(Man.—Ch. III.-l. 52).

5 கூந்த லேந்து சாயலார்

இங்கிதக் களிப்பினு லெய்தியாடும் பூம்பொழில்

(Cin.—v.-145).

were wide and long. The other streets were either wide or narrow. The narrow lanes (கோணம்) and the big streets (மறுகு) were cut on a definite plan in the contour in accordance with the rules laid down in the Śāstras. [6]

Śāstras do not contemplate a uniform row of streets equal in length and width, but there may be narrow lanes as well as big streets, as the topography and other conditions permit.

*Public halls.*

The chief public place in a city (ஊரம்பலம்) is the building left solely for the use of travellers. Such places where people stay for some time were kept in good sanitary condition. There were also special [7] halls left for the exclusive use of ascetics. The ambalam or the theatre where dramas were staged, was another public place which was well maintained.

---

6 விதிக்கிடைகாணலாம் வீதிமா நகர்

(Cin.—v.-1999).

7 பாங்கர் மாதவம் புரிகுநர் சாலைகள் பலவால்

(Kanda.—Nak. v.-35)

Public schools and other manṛams (Ch. X) were likewise kept in good condition.

There were also public playgrounds where young men played at ball, which resembled in a way modern Association Football or Rugby. Such young men played at different games in the open spaces provided for their use. It is said [8] that they would sometimes carry a ball placed on the ground; and that at other times they would either thump it with the hand or kick it with force or hide it somewhere.

*Tanks.*

Much attention was paid to the proper maintenance of public baths and drinking water tanks. Persons affected with bodily infirmities took their baths in tanks noted for the valuable curative properties of the water. Several tanks were dug out in a city or a village, each shrine being

8 வைத்தபந்தெடுத்தலும் மாலையுட்கரத்தலுங்
கைத்தலத்தி னோட்டலுங் கண்ணி நெற்றி தீட்ட
லும்
பத்தியிற் புடைத்தலும் பைய ரவ்வி னோடலும்
இத்திறத்த பந்தி னோடின்ப மெல்லையில்லையே
(Cin.—v.-151).

associated with a number of Tirthams or bathing tanks which were kept in good sanitary condition. Gardens on the bunds of the tank, and the lotus, violet and other flowering plants in the water added an additional charm and beauty [9] to such tanks which were used for bathing purposes. The light reflected from every tree and flower near a stream or a tank augment the general effect of the sunshine which pours from the sky on the sheet of water. This has been a theme for the poets. Such tanks were dug deep and wide and water flowers were cultivated in them. In these deep tanks there were big fishes [10] which ensured the purity of the water.

Among the essentials of a habitable village, good water supply was given the foremost importance. As the Poetess

---

9 காலுற நிமிர்ந்திடு காமர் சோலையும்
நீலமுங் கமலமு நிறைந்த பொய்கையும்

(Kanda.—Nat. v.-30).

10 நிலையருந்துட்ட நோக்கி நெடி திருந்து
புலவுக்கய லெடுத்த

(Sir.—l.-180-181).

Avvaiyār tersely put [11] it 'Reside in a place where there is plenty of water'. Hence it is that villages rapidly grew along the banks of rivers. A riverside ensures good water supply. The æsthetic excellence of a river adjoining a village has been emphasised by the Poetess who states [12] "A place without a river is a dreary waste." In addition to such tanks, deep wells also were constructed [13] with a flight of steps leading to them. The lotus and other water flowers were cultivated in these wells which were used for bathing. The fresh water tanks containing water for drinking purposes were known as ūruṇi (from ūruṇ-nir, three words meaning the drinking water tank [14] common to the village). Such tanks were dug out in the centre of a town or a village.

---

11 நீரகம்பொருந்திய ஊரகத்திரு (Kon.).

12 ஆறில்லா ஊருக்கழகுபாழ் (Nv.).

13 நன்மலர் நாணவாவி நீரணி நயந்தும் (Cin.—v. 2840).

14 ஊருணியொத்த பொதுவாய் (Kall.—v.-57).

Hence the house-wife had not to go a long way to fetch drinking water. The governing principles in the maintenance of Ūruṇis, are their purity, their usefulness, and their easy accessibility. The Ūruṇi was dug out generally in a central locality which was rendered more beautiful by the growth of trees around and by the row of well kept houses abutting in front of it.

The central fresh water tank was always very welcome to the people. The author of the Kuṛal[15] compares the wealth in the hands of the liberal minded men to the water in the central tank, and observes that just as the water in the Ūruṇi is useful to all, so also the money in the possession of those who are charitably disposed would be available to every one in need. It was usual to grow trees of medicinal value along the bunds of the fresh water tanks. The three fruit trees, the Indian gall-nut, nelli, and tānṛi (கடு,

---

15 ஊருணி நீர்நிறைந் தற்றே யுலகவாம்
பேரறி வாளன் றிரு

(Kurl.—v.-215).

நெல்லி, தான்றி) were generally planted all along the bund of such tanks. These trees yield fruits which are the simple remedies for various ailments.

The principle which underlies the planting of such trees on the bunds of tanks is easily intelligible. Trees hold up the water level which would fall without them. Hence the presence of trees near the tank was very useful. Moreover, the fruits of these trees contain some tannin in them. This tannin adds a slight sweet taste to the water and thus masks any excess of chlorine in drinking water. It is also useful in clearing the water of its impurities on the surface, by carrying down to the bottom all dirt and clay that the water may contain, thus serving the same purpose as alum added to muddy water. Hence the ancients generally planted these trees near the bunds of drinking water tanks.

In public feeding places and in private homes the water of such tanks was used with resultant benefit to health and comfort.[16] This crystal water of high medicinal value was always taken in pots and kept in houses and was used for even ordinary purposes.[17]

Such tanks had an inlet for incoming fresh water and an outlet for discharging extra water. It was considered very important that the[18] inlet and the outlet should be well kept. People rejoiced in seeing the central tank filled with fresh water. So great is the inborn pleasure and delight at the sight of a plentiful supply of good water, that in South India, feasts are held even to day to commemorate the coming in of freshes in the river. When the Emperor Daśarata broke the news of his abdication in favour of his eldest son Rama, and wished to know how the installation of Rama on the throne

---

16 விலக்கில் சாலை யாவர்க்கும் வெப்பின் முப்பழச் சுனை
தலைத்தண்ணீர்...

(Cin.—v.-75).

17 முப்பழ நீர்............ தாமரைக்கண் கழீஇயினான்

(Cin.—v.-2356).

18 தூம்பியாது மில்லாக்குளம் போல்

(Cin.—v.-1976).

would be welcomed by the people, the sages, and ministers replied "Whoever would set his face against *filling the central tank with fresh water* or look with feelings other than those of delight and pleasure at the *ripening of the fruits in the central fruit tree*? If rains come in season and bring freshes in a river which fills all irrigation sources, people would certainly rejoice in such an event. Even so, they would now receive the news of the installation of Rama on the throne. They look upon Rama with greater love and attachment than they regard their *drinking water* or their very lives."[19]

These are evidences to show the extent to which public conscience was educated in ancient times on such public health questions as the provision of good water supply, parks and open spaces. And even

---

19 ஊருணி நிறையவு முதவுமாடுயர்
பார்கெழு பழுமரம் பழுத்தற் றாகவும்
கார்மழை பொழியவுங் கழனி பாய்நதி
வார்புனல் பெருகவு மறுக்கின்றார்கள் யார்
(Kam.—II-1.-v.-82).
உண்ணுநீரினு முயிரினு மவனை யேயுவப்பார்
Do.—v.-40).

to-day are to be seen several such central tanks (ஊருணி) in different parts of South India. If these tanks are well maintained, they would form very useful sources of good water supply to the villages where they are situated. As an instance of one such Ūruṇi kept in very good condition now and under proper supervision, may be mentioned the big Ūruṇi in the town of Ramnad with a flower garden on one side of it. This is situated most beautifully in the centre of the town and the houses abutting in front of it present a most fascinating sight.

*Houses.*

The general principle in the construction of houses was that it should not be too big. As the Poetess Avvaiyār has expressed in a pithy saying, [20] "Do not build too large a house". The small house is attractive from an artistic point of view. It gives an opportunity of getting charming effects in a small space. Moreover economy in a house is a matter of very great

20 இடம்பட வீடிடேல்

(Ac.).

importance. Expenditure on a house is a recurring one. It is an expense that goes constantly on, and according to the size of the house will be the annual charges of repairing, whitewashing, renewing the woodwork and all other costs of maintaining it in good condition.

The kitchen should be spaciously constructed. (அகன் அட்டில்.) A house should have several apartments and divisions. The front hall known as Kūḍam is otherwise called Śāvaḍi or an open space where all may be received. The other apartments would be behind this portion. The utility of the Śāvaḍi is that it screens [21] the rear portion of a house from public gaze. In a decent house there would be a pial inside, where the ladies of the household may sit behind the screen afforded by the Kūḍam or the first compartment of the house.

The pials in front of the house should be spacious. Artistic figures may be worked in

---

21 கூடம் இல் மறைவு

(Nik.).

the threshold and in the doors. A flight[22] of steps would lead up to the pial and front of houses. This suggests an elevated ground for constructing a house. The different divisions in the house as the first portion, second portion, etc., were intended to accommodate a growing joint family. The better class of houses were provided with decent pials and sloping backs, the whole being plastered over in colour.[23]

### *Home Pride.*

A house which gives happiness to its owners and to those who live in it has an air of rejoicing. The love of home is so deep-rooted in the minds of the people that even when the roof is leaky and the house is rendered otherwise useless for occupation, the owners would still stick on to their old homes, and bale out by

---

22 குறுந்தொடை நெடும்படிக்காற்
கொடுந்திண்ணைப் பஃறகைப்பிற்
புழைவாயிற் போகிடைகழி

(Pattin.—l.-142-144).

23 குங்குமமெழுகிச் சார்வுந்திண்ணையுங்குயிற்றி

(Cin.—v.-108).

buckets if necessary, the rain water pouring in through an old roof.[24] To them its rooms are like companions, for in them abide memories that years cannot disturb. The very old walls constructed in a previous generation bring to their minds vivid experiences of the past and they are therefore dear and precious to them. They would not easily part from such old homes.

*Ownership of a House.*

As a house is such a valuable possession, it is only fitting that it should be secured as personal property. It is an enrichment of life to possess one's own house. The man who has no house of his own is not generally regarded. "He has not got even a shelter" is a common saying to indicate the imprudence of a man. Every man is therefore enjoined to secure a small house for himself.[25] The ownership of a house brings security and

---

24 செறிப்பில் பழங்கூரை சேறணை யாக
இறைத்துநீ ரேற்றுங் கிடப்பர்

(Nal.—v.-231).

25 "வீடாவாசலா"; "சாண்நிழலாவதுவேண்டும்."

comfort. It is such ownership which gives pleasure and pride in the house without which the house will very soon dilapidate. It is a common idea that houses unoccupied for a long time are of the same nature as human bodies without a Soul. They become the prey of every gloomy spirit. And people believe that such houses are haunted by evil spirits and as such unworthy of occupation.

These facts suggest the principle that the ownership of a house and actual occupation of it by the person who built it, should be encouraged. But one must remember that there are few things more exciting than the building of a house. The anticipation of having our own house is *per se* a pleasurable excitement. As the old saying [26] goes, it is as exciting as arranging for a marriage. There are many practical difficulties to be got over. First to choose the site for it, to get the best outlook for the windows and the entrance, and to take into account the

---

26 கல்யாணத்தைப்பண்ணிப்பார் வீட்டைக்கட்டிப்பார்.

neighbouring houses and get our own into right relations with them; secondly, to make up one's mind about the size of the house, and the money to be spent upon it; and thirdly, to discuss the plan and get immersed in practical details take up considerable time and thought. And yet even with so much forethought, one finds that unless he can spend at least twice if not thrice his original estimate, he will have to abandon one after another many of his cherished fancies.

### *Children.*

In the houses of rich people the courtyards were always very spacious and airy. This open space would be useful to the children who play here.[27] It is stated that in such open courtyards the children learnt to walk with the help of the three-wheeled go-cart. Even in the smaller houses of the poor, the children romped about in the streets and in the open.

---

27 பொற்காற் புதல்வர் புரவியின் றுருட்டும்
முக்காற் சிறுதேர் முன்வழி விலக்கும்.

(Pattin.—1.-24-25.)

It is a truism to state that the conditions under which the early years of life are lived, determine to a very large extent the physical, mental and moral health of a race. The children should therefore have space freedom and ample room to stretch their limbs and play about without restriction. The miserable slouch and cowardly gait and look which distinguish some school children, indicate most prominently the absence of such desirable space freedom in their houses. Healthy environment is very much appreciated by the children. And hence the courtyard specially appeals to them as an open space where they might spend most of their time. Without a courtyard or other open space, the home is of no use as it does not provide suitable health conditions for the growth of the child.

The home is chiefly important on account of the children living in it. As the Poetess Avvaiyār says,[28] " The child'

---

28 மைந்தன்மனைக்குமணி.

(Nvb.).

is the ornament of the home." If then the home should fulfil its highest function of becoming a centre of early education and social life for the children, the courtyard, the garden, the pial and other spaces should be there to enable the children to live and grow under the influence of bright sunshine and air. The courtyard with the Tuḷasi plant in it not only affords physical advantages to the growing child but it is at the same time an important spiritual influence as well.

### *Sea-Side.*

The sea-side was generally beautified by paths with flower plants on either side. There were also some bowers and retreats of Punnai and Tāḻai trees. The flower of the Punnai is specially noted for its superb fragrance. The tree flourishes in sandy soil. Its smell[29] keeps off the bad odour of fish on the sea-shore. Such simple devices actuated by common sense considerations contributed to the sanitary condition of the locality.

---

29 கயற்புலால், புன்னைகடியும் பொருகடற்றண்சேர்ப்ப (Nal.—v.-97).

## *Drainage.*

The disposal of waste water was well regulated. There was a system [30] of drainage by which all the water used for domestic purposes found their way by means of sluices into the ditch outside the city. The accumulation of mud and dirt in the streets was washed through side openings into the sub-ways and conveyed with the sewage to a destination outside the city. The water passed through canals covered over with stones. (Curuṅgu or கரந்துகற்படை)

There was a ditch round each portion of the city already described as Akanakar, Iḍainakar, and Puṛanakar. The water used in houses found its way into the channels by means of drains. This emptied itself into a ditch which was connected with the ditches of the other divisions of the city. Thus all the water

---

30 நீணிலம் வகுத்துநீர் நிரந்துவந் திழிதரச்
சேணிலற்றியற்றிய சித்திரச் சுருங்கைசேர்
கோணிலத்துவெய்ய வாங்கொடுஞ் சுறத்தடங்
கிடங்கு
(Cin.—v.-142).

used in a city was led into the main ditch. And by rearing trees on the sides of the ditch and allowing water flowers like the lotus to grow in the water, a use was found for this waste water which thus fertilised the trees on the banks.

The ditch was நானக்கிடங்கு (Cin-v.590). The water used for bathing purposes in private houses was led into it by a good system of drainage. It was very deep and filled with fish. It was thus a pool of retreat which received all the waste water of private houses and of the streets of the town.

In places where there was no ditch but a natural run of drainage towards the sea or a big river, the water was led by drainage canals [31] into the sea or other big tank outside the city. By this means the bad effects of a stationary drain water were avoided.

*A Comprehensive Scheme.*

It would thus be clear that the planning of Indian cities was no haphazard growth

---

31 ஊரங்கணநீர் உரவுநீர்ச்சேர்ந்தக்கால்
(Nal.—v.-175).

of mere chance. An intelligent effort seems to have been made to secure a systematic lay-out on the most approved ideas of sanitary condition and convenience for the people occupying the villages and towns. We gather from the Skānda-purāṇa that when Śūran (supposed to be a Demon) asked Brahma to rebuild his city which was destroyed by an enemy, he requested that the lay-out may be orderly and well-thought-out, that the houses, streets, towers, gardens, maṇḍa-pams, tanks, public halls, theatres and platforms be all well planned in the projected town plan.[32]

Such pre-arranged design is a distinct feature of the villages with temples and of cities with temples and palaces.

These simple rules ensured proper sanitary conditions and an orderly growth

---

32 பொன்மதின்மாடவீதி பொலன்மணிச்சிகரம் வேர
மன்மதன் விழையுஞ்சோலை மண்டபம் வாவி
பொய்கை
சென்மலியரங்கமன்றம் தெற்றியேமுதலவெல்லாம்
தொன்மைபோலாகத் தன்கைத்தொழின்முறை
படைத்தான் மன்னோ
(Kanda.—C.-v.-26).

of houses so that when the town is definitely planned as a whole, it was not left to grow in a chaotic manner. And while the details were modified here and there according to local circumstances and needs, the underlying principles were everywhere the same. They always combined æsthetic and hygienic considerations in village or town planning.

*Conclusion.*

Thus a critical study of the literature of the country would prove to be of great benefit to the future town planner.

The cities like Kāvērippūmpaṭṭinam would provide valuable suggestions worth our earnest attention.

The climatic conditions of India, and the spiritual and the material needs of the millions inhabiting the vast Peninsula have to be borne in mind in designing future towns and villages, or in improving or developing the existing conditions. Every new plan should be adopted to village life with its characteristic Indian customs and Indian requirements.

It was because such ideas were faithfully preserved in the plan that the ancient cities like Madura and Conjeeveram are still the wonder and admiration of all.

The older Tamil literature is a faithful record of the history and civilization of the ancient Dekkan, and is therefore very useful as enabling us to live over in imagination the life of the ancient people of this land and draw therefrom valuable suggestions which are well worth adopting even to-day.

# BOOKS BY THE AUTHOR.

**I.—Kamban and his Art.**—A Monograph in English on the author of the Ramayana in Tamil with an Introduction by the *Hon'ble Mr. Justice T. V. Seshagiri Ayyar*, Madras. (General Trading Co., Cuddalore N.T.) Re. 1.

*The Madras Mail.*—The book must be welcome to many who are unacquainted with Tamil and who therefore could not realise the ennobling influence of his great works of immortal literary excellence. The author brings out the outstanding merits of Kamban as a poet and his wonderful powers of realistic description and of rousing the imagination, and appealing to the emotions.

*The Modern Review, Calcutta*—Whatever our friends of Madras set their hands on they do in a thorough-going fashion. There is no English appreciation of any Bengali poet for instance to match this production. The author's admiration for Vernacular literature is highly commendable

*Dr. Sir S. Subramania Ayyar.*—It is very gratifying to find among our *alumni* one so capable like yourself of doing justice to the genius of the greatest Tamil Poet. Your pamphlet is so thorough as to leave little to be desired in bringing to the notice of your readers the excellence of the Ramayanam.

*Dr. Rash Behari Ghose.*—A very interesting monograph which shows that Kamban was not only a great poet but also a great and good man of whom every Tamilian has a right to be proud.

*C. Srikanta, Litt., D., Colombo.*—I must congratulate you on having written such a fascinating book which well deserves to be read by all lovers of Kamban's Ramayanam.

## BOOKS BY THE AUTHOR.

*M. R. Ry. J. Ramayya Pantulu Garu.*—At a time when people see nothing worthy in their Vernacular literatures you have done a patriotic act in drawing attention to the merits of the Tamil national poet and it is to be hoped that your book will open the eyes of the sceptics.

*Dr. L. D. Barnett, British Museum, London.*—It is a most attractive study of the poet.

**II.—Youth and Character.**—A Text Book of Moral Instruction in Tamil suitable for the young.—A delightful story of Two Boys on the model of Sandford and Merton, and suited to the requirements of Indian conditions. (Macmillan & Co.) Price As. 8.

*The Madras Mail.*—A Moral Text Book of exceptional interest and value.

*The Hindu.*—The style is racy and fluent, simple and expressive and the illustrative stories told in it may be advantageously read even by elderly people. Books of this kind ought to be welcomed. They serve as models for study and composition.

*The Hon'ble Mr. Justice T. V. Seshagiri Ayyar.*—It is written in simple easy Tamil. There is absolutely no pedantry about it; and the topics introduced are such as ought to appeal to the good instincts of school children.

**III.—A Critical Study of Tirumurukarruppadai.**—(A literary and critical estimate in Tamil of an ancient religious poem in praise of God Subramanya), (C. Coomarasawmy Nayudu & Sons, Madras). As. 4.

**IV.—Town Planning in Ancient Dekkan.**—With an Introduction by *Professor Patrick Geddes.* (An exposition in English of the principles of Town Planning as they are reflected in the classic Tamil literature); with three illustrations. Rs. 2. (General Trading Co. Cuddalore N.T.)